SHATTERED
BUT
NOT BROKEN

MY STORY OF LIFETIME SPOUSAL ABUSE
AND THE LONG ROAD
OF SURVIVAL AND RECOVERY

TAWANA J CAMPBELL

Jan-Carol
Publishing, Inc
"every story needs a book"

SHATTERED
BUT NOT BROKEN
Tawana J Campbell

Published June 2014
Express Editions
Imprint of Jan-Carol Publishing, Inc
All rights reserved
Copyright © 2014 by Tawana J Campbell
Front Cover and Book Design: Tara Sizemore

ISBN: 978-1-939289-42-1
Library of Congress Control Number: 2014942797

You may contact the publisher:
Jan-Carol Publishing, Inc
PO Box 701
Johnson City, TN 37605
E-mail: publisher@jancarolpublishing.com
jancarolpublishing.com

To my wonderful family;
to my best friend, Dee;
and to my wonderful Auntie—
you were always there for me
and never left my side.
Thank you, thank you!

Letter to the Reader

By the grace of God, I endured and have triumphed over 34 years of fear, pain, discouragement, and loss due to spousal abuse. Although I feel that God led me to write *Shattered But Not Broken*, I have to confess that it took me almost 12 years to do so—in part because I was reluctant to go back and relive those dark times. However, going back has enabled me to go forward. I hope that, by reading my story, other women—and men—in abusive relationships realize that they too can reach the end of the long road of survival and recovery. I hope that you feel the anointing from each page and that it lets you know that God is there for you. And no matter your life circumstances, remember—*you are somebody.*

Sincerely,

Jawana

Acknowledgements

I thank God for carrying me through one of the most difficult times of my life. And I thank God for giving me a sound mind—without which I wouldn't have been able to write this book. Thank you, Lord, also for the gift of a heart filled with love—and with the peace that surpasses all understanding (Philippians 4:7).

FOREWORD

THURSDAY, AUGUST 28, 1989
9:30 AM

My husband and I were going through our morning routine—drinking coffee and scanning the newspaper—as we waited for the phone to ring. James hadn't been feeling well for a while, so we called to make a doctor's appointment for that morning. The receptionist said she'd call back once she had a time worked out. The phone rang, and expecting it to be the doctor's office, I picked up. Instead I was surprised. On the line was the voice of someone I didn't recognize, the voice of a young girl with an accent. She asked to speak to James. And with that brief, unexpected phone call, my life was changed forever.

CHAPTER 1

FALL 1966

It's October 31, 1966, Halloween Day. Young teenage girls, my friend and I were walking around the neighborhood. We enjoyed walking together, just looking at things and people. On this day, we were checking out houses that we wanted to visit for trick-or-treating that night. We had been walking around what we considered to be a big block, when a car with a couple of guys drove up beside of us. My friend recognized the driver, but neither one of us recognized the passenger in the car.

The driver, being her friend, introduced us to his passenger. "I want you to meet my cousin, James," he said. "He's on vacation and will be visiting for a while."

Yes, it was love at first sight for me. I knew that I loved him the moment I saw him. He was the most handsome man I had ever seen. I knew in my heart that he was the one. As they drove away, I looked to my friend and said very methodically, "I am going to marry James one day."

She looked at me with disbelief and shock.

On our way back home, she and I talked about James—his good looks and how I was so sure that he was the one who I would marry one day. My friend was as excited as I was. It was two schoolgirls with a fantasy, with a schoolgirl crush on an older boy.

When I arrived home, I ran into the house to tell Mom that I met the man who I was going to marry. Mom was busy in the kitchen, and I burst through the door and announced, "Mom, I just met the guy I am going to marry! He has Elvis Presley's good looks. And one day I am going to marry him!"

Mom's reaction was total disbelief. "Sure you are," she said with a smile. She went back to her cooking and asked, "What's his name?"

"His name is James, and one day I will marry him. You'll see."

I didn't sleep much that night. I was too excited. James was on my mind. All day at school, I was lost in my thoughts about James. *How am I going to get in touch with him? I don't even know his last name!*

After school that afternoon, I called my friend to go for a walk in the neighborhood.

"How do you think that I can get in touch with James?" I asked her.

"Gee, I don't know."

We had walked in silence for a while, when we heard a car driving up beside of us. We turned, and it was the driver—the friend, James's cousin. He was alone, but it gave us the opportunity to ask questions.

So many questions needing so many answers! But what I heard, I could not believe. We learned that James was visiting his family, staying with his brother on the other side of town. But the biggest surprise was that I knew James's sister and had known her for some time. His sister and her husband were part of a group of friends who got together and played music. But most importantly, I learned that James was a bachelor.

I know many people do not believe in love at first sight, especially for a teenager, but there was something different about this whole situation. I could not put my finger on it, but I somehow knew he was the one. Of course as a teenager, I dreamed of meeting my Prince Charming who would sweep me away with him. With each passing day, I felt that I had met my Prince Charming. I felt myself falling more in love with James. *Can this really be happening? Is this real love or just a teenage crush and something of my imagination?*

I was raised in Small Town, USA, in a blue-collar, working-class family. Dad was a truck driver and was always on the road. It seemed that he was always gone. As a small child, I wanted Dad to be around for special events but understood that being gone was part of his job. The responsibly of raising the children was on my mom's shoulders. As the oldest of five children, with two sisters and two brothers, Mom depended on us to help with household chores. Because we depended on each other, we were all very close.

We were raised in a good Christian environment with Christian values, all of which I am very proud of today. Those Christian values and my strong faith are what brought me through the most devastating situations of my life.

In a short few days, on November 15, I was going to be sixteen years old. Do you remember how it was to be sixteen? I felt so grown up, and I knew what I wanted in life and what I wanted to do with my life. I wanted to be the perfect wife to a wonderful husband. I knew that I had met my man when I met James. He was older and more mature. I was never interested in anyone my age or younger, so finding out that James was twenty-two years old just confirmed he was the one for me.

With each passing day, I became more obsessed with my thoughts of James. I was very much surprised at school one day when I found out from a classmate that he was actually a neighbor of James's.

"I want to send a message to James. Will you take a note to him for me?" I asked.

"Sure," he said.

I took out a piece of paper and wrote something like this:

Hi, my name is Tawana. I am the girl you met the other day when you and your cousin drove by. I sure do think that you are a nice-looking guy, and I was wondering if you could write back to me.

My classmate took the note and agreed to give it to James. I was so excited and worried at the same time. *What if I don't hear from him? Will he be interested in a girl like me? Will he really write back, or will this be the end of my first true love?*

That afternoon, I called my friend to go walking in the neighborhood. I just needed to talk to someone. I could not wait to tell her. "I sent a note to James today," I said with excitement. "Do you think that was okay?"

"Sure, why not? I think that it was okay," she said with a smile. "Who knows? Don't forget, we are going to Homecoming, aren't we? The homecoming game is on November 12, and one of the candidates for Queen wants us to be there."

"Oh yes!" I answered her as my mind wondered back to James. *What a dream to come true if I could go to the game with James!*

That night I couldn't sleep. I was so excited with anticipation. *Will James reply to my note? Will he write me back? What will he say?* I headed to school early the next morning.

My classmate handed me a note. "James told me to give this to you."

James had written back to me! I was so nervous and shaking, I had to hold the letter with both hands to read it.

Hi, I think that you are a pretty girl. I would like to come by your house to see you.

I was so excited. I asked my classmate to take my reply to James, and he agreed. I wrote so quickly that I was surprised that anyone could read it.

Hi, James—If you can, come by the house this evening.

My excitement was almost uncontainable on so many levels. First, James stated he thought that I was pretty. Being overweight and develop-ing earlier than most teenage girls, I did not receive many compliments. *WOW! James thinks that I'm pretty!* I was totally swept off my feet. Second, he asked to see me. That was my plan! I wanted James to come and see me.

I rushed home from school and announced to Mom, "James is coming over this evening to see me!"

"Who is James?" Mom asked.

"I told you! The man who I am going to marry!" I said.

"You're kidding, aren't you?" Mom asked with total shock and surprise.

"NO!" I shouted. "I've got to wash my hair and decide what I am going to wear! I have to pick out the perfect outfit. He will be here! And Mom, he looks just like Elvis! He is really good-looking!"

"Dinner will be ready soon," Mom said with a grin.

"I'm too nervous. No dinner for me. I've got to get dressed!" I made my way to my bedroom to get dressed for my prince.

Time seemed to stand still, but somehow the clock finally showed 6:30 pm, and my Prince Charming had not arrived. Just as I looked the clock with a sinking feeling, I heard a car. I looked out the front door, and here coming up the driveway was a 1958 soft green and white Pontiac. It was James. I thought, *I am going to pass out!*

I didn't pass out. He got out of the car and walked to the door. My brothers and sisters gave him a warm welcome. We were all excited, and after all of us calmed down, we sat down and started talking about everyday things. It was so natural.

James told us that he was from Kentucky, where his family still lived. He had a large family. He was a middle child among thirteen siblings, seven older and seven younger. His Dad worked as a coalminer. James had a couple of sisters and a brother living in Indiana and had recently visited them. It was such an easy evening, and we really enjoyed it. Talking was smooth. My mind moved forward to the homecoming game, which was just a week away. I thought, *Why not?*

"James, the homecoming game and the Homecoming Queen contest are on the 12th. Would you like to go?" I asked trying not to show my nervousness and being over anxious.

As I studied his face, he answered with a smile, "Sure, I'd like to go. We all can go. I'll take you and your sisters. What about your brothers?"

"They're too young to go unless we ask Mom if it's okay to go. But I'll ask," I said.

It was getting late, and James said his goodbyes. When he left, I told Mom how much I enjoyed talking with James and how I found him to be so nice.

"James offered to take us all to the game. Can the boys go too?" I asked.

"I have to think about that. We did just meet James," Mom said with a wink.

"But it's just a week before the game," I said.

"With your Dad not home, I'll have to wait and discuss it with him."

I thought, *Dad will say no.* Somehow I knew deep down inside that he would say no. We had never been allowed to go to the school games or to participate in anything at school.

I woke up on Friday morning thinking about Dad coming home. He was usually home on the weekends, so we always tried to cram everything into those two days. It was natural that all of us tried to discuss things with him and to share our week's happenings. It was an exciting time for us when Dad arrived home after being gone all week.

By the time I got home from school, Dad had called and told Mom where to meet him. Mom and all of us kids loaded into the car, and off we went to meet Dad. We all loved him very much, and going to pick him up was a family thing to do. We shared it. By the time we got back home, everything was back to normal, like Dad had never been away.

As we drove to pick up Dad, I asked Mom, "Are you going to ask Dad for me?"

"And what would that be?" she asked teasingly.

"You know. The game and James!" I quickly replied.

"Oh that!" she said with a wink.

All seemed normal, but Mom never indicated one way or the other that she had discussed anything with Dad all weekend. By Sunday morning, as we were on our way to Sunday School, I still wondered if Dad had given his permission. I wasn't even sure that Mom had discussed it with Dad.

On Sunday night after church, we started to take Dad back to the truck for him to be gone all week. I still didn't know his answer. I decided that I had to know.

"Dad, are you going to let us go?" I asked without warning.

"Let you go where?" Dad asked.

My heart fell. Mom had not asked him. "Did Mom not ask you?" I asked in a low, disappointed tone.

He smiled and said, "Yes, she did. And yes, you can go."

I couldn't believe my ears! My sisters and I started screaming, "YES! YES! YES!" I was so excited. The game was Thursday night, and I was going on my first date with James!

On Monday, my classmate took a note to James to tell him that I, along with my siblings, could go with him to the game.

Later that evening, James came over to visit. James was a sight to behold! He lifted weights, and my two brothers thought that was super to have muscles as large as James's. Of course, my sisters were as excited as I was to have James visit. It seemed very natural for James to start visiting every night, after I got home from school.

I was having strong feelings for James. It was obvious to me. This feeling deep down inside that I couldn't explain to myself or anyone else told me that I was falling in love with him. I could only hope that he was having the same feelings for me.

Thursday night finally arrived. We were all going to the game—my sisters, my close girlfriend, and I. James picked us up at the house and away we went.

That night was like a dream. The date, the game, and our neighbor winning the Homecoming Queen contest. What a wonderful time we had! I just had a feeling that everything would work out for James and me. I just knew that he was the one and that it was meant to be.

***

On the following morning, Friday morning, James sent a note to me by our mutual friend. His note read:

Would you like to go like to go to supper with me tonight? I will come by and pick you up.

On this Friday, Dad had arrived home early. So, I when got home from school, Dad was already there. As nervous as I was, I knew that I had to ask Dad, or at least let Dad know that James was on his way to see me.

"Dad, James is coming over, and he wants to take me out to supper," I said in a quivering tone.

"Young lady, I don't think that you should go," Dad said without hesitation.

I was devastated. My heart as well as my lower lip hit the floor.

"Oh, please Dad, let me go! I'll take the girls with us. Oh Dad, oh please," I pleaded.

Dad didn't answer.

I had to think that it would be all right. I went to my room and got dressed as if I knew that I was allowed to go with James.

Just as planned, James arrived on time. He knocked at the door, and I ran to welcome him. Dad was sitting in the living room, and I greeted James at the door and invited him in. I still didn't know for sure if Dad was going to grant me permission to go with James.

James came inside and immediately began to talk to Dad. They talked and talked. I just watched and listened. Finally Dad said, "I guess you two want to go to supper. Well, you can go—on one condition."

My heart fell to the floor again. I looked at Dad and asked, "What condition?"

Dad replied, "That we all go. Me, your mom, and all of us. We ain't had supper either!"

I was just relieved that I could go, I didn't care if the whole family went with James and me. I was excited to be with James, and that's all that mattered to me.

Unsure of what James thought, I answered, "That's fine. We all can go."

So, all of us, including my four siblings, hopped in the car with James. It really didn't seem to bother James. He was used to a large family, so he didn't care. This acceptance and attitude of his just made me love him more.

***

During the evening, I told James about my birthday party that was planned for the next day, on Saturday. Mom and Dad had agreed that I could invite a lot of my friends from school, including boys and girls. With Dad being home, I was hoping to have a fun party. I was excited about my birthday party. *But*, I thought, *to make my birthday party special, I'd love to have James attend.* I had to find the courage to ask him.

"I'm having my sixteenth birthday party tomorrow night. Do you think that you can come?" I asked him with great anticipation.

James smiled and said, "I'd love to."

I just couldn't believe it. James was going to come to my birthday party. *This will be best-ever birthday party!*

I invited all my classmates to my birthday. Little did I know that at my birthday party, the same thing that happened to me, with 'falling in love' at first sight, was going to happen to my sister. She was about to meet the man she would marry. There was a boy in my class who had the attention of one of my girlfriends. However, my sister said that she wanted to meet him. I invited him to the party and introduced him to my sister. It was love at first sight for them too. My sister was fourteen, and he was sixteen. She was in love, and I was in love. We both had found our Prince Charmings. That was the best night of our young lives.

For my birthday, James bought me a very pretty necklace, a jewelry box, and a beautiful mohair sweater. I had the perfect skirt to go with the sweater, which I wanted to wear all the time. I even made sure that I had a picture of James and me, with me wearing my favorite outfit.

The Thanksgiving holiday came quickly. I started to wonder how James was planning to spend his holiday—with me or his family. It seemed simpler if he decided to go visit his family, because I would be spending the holiday with my family. We always visited my maternal grandparents during Thanksgiving. It was a joyous time, and I hoped that James would visit me during the holidays, but I had to understand if he did not.

"Mom, if James decides to stays around for Thanksgiving, can he go with us to visit Grandma and Grandpa?" I asked with uncertainty.

"Don't you think that James will go visit his own family?" Mom asked.

"I don't know. But if he doesn't, can he go with us?" I asked again.

"If he wants to," Mom answered, "I don't see why not."

As it turned out, James did not go out of town, and he joined us for Thanksgiving. He was like a member of the family. When it came time to go to my grandparents, we all went together, including James. We laughed and sang songs. It was so natural, and we had a wonderful time. When we got there, there were more of my relatives. All my aunts and uncles were there as well. It was like a family reunion at The Old Home Place', but with one addition to the family—James. James was a good fit in our family, and we had so much fun. Even though James was seven years older than I, it didn't seem to matter. I was so thankful that my family had accepted James and that James had accepted my family.

Thinking ahead, I knew that Christmas might mean that James would be going home for the holiday, especially since he had been with me for Thanksgiving. I knew that it would be okay though, because Thanksgiving was the best ever!

CHAPTER 2

It was the first week of December, and things were going very well. Christmas lights and tree decorations were everywhere. It was beginning to look like Christmas everywhere we went.

In the meantime, James has taken a new job with the same company where his brother-in-law worked. James had moved to Indiana from New Jersey, where a brother and other relatives of his lived. But once James got that job here, he was ready to settle down. He liked his new job, and it gave him roots here.

Our communication to each other continued with sending letters by our mutual friend. We were now sealing our notes in envelopes so that he couldn't read them. We are getting more involved and didn't want our courier to read our letters. Our notes were much more serious. We had started to talk about a long-term relationship and to hint about future things that we would do together. We even discussed shopping for gifts for our families as if were already in a committed relationship.

It was around the middle of December, and we had planned to go on a date and do some Christmas shopping. When we stopped to get a bite to eat, James said, "You know, I think that we should think about what we will do when we get married."

I was in shock. *Marriage? We're talking about marriage?*

"James, you have to talk to Dad about us getting married. You know that, don't you?" I asked, thinking that I was going to faint. This was all I had ever dreamed of having. I wanted to be married to a handsome man, and I would be the best wife ever. I guess I was 'in love' like most young girls, but during this timeframe and given my background and generation, marriage was accepted for someone young as I. It was more than accepted—it was expected.

"Dad won't be home until tomorrow," I nervously said.

"I'll ask him then," James said.

We both agreed that I should discuss things with Mom and that he would discuss our getting married with Dad tomorrow.

I was so nervous. I thought my heart would burst with excitement.

I couldn't think of anything else. We came home from shopping that evening, and I was very anxious when James left. I knew that I had to discuss it with Mom.

When James left, I walked into the kitchen where Mom was having a cup of coffee. "Mom," I said. Then—without warning—I started crying.

"Are you all right?" Mom asked.

"James wants to get married," I replied through tears. "He wants to discuss it with Dad tomorrow."

Mom did not seem surprised. She smiled, "I understand how you feel. I felt the same way when your Dad wanted to marry me."

Since Dad was five years older than Mom and since she had married at a young age, it didn't see like a bad thing for me to do the same. It seemed like it was a natural progression in life. Like I was doing, this was what most of us girls talked about—meeting the man of our dreams and getting married, having children, and being a housewife. This was what Mom had done, what her mom had done—it was tradition.

Dad arrived home late Friday night, so on Saturday morning, Mom was keeping us kids as quiet as possible to let him sleep in. I wanted Dad to be rested, because, after all, I expected a big day ahead of me. *I surely don't want anything going wrong today!*

We went through the day as normal. I told my brothers and sisters that James was going to talk to Dad and that we had some big news. They were very excited and didn't want anything to happen to upset Dad. They loved

James almost much as I did. And deep down inside, I believed that Dad liked James too.

By mid-afternoon, Dad was up and was hungry.

"Hey, do you want to get something to eat?"

"Yes!" we all said together. We were so excited to go out with Mom and Dad, but I was especially excited. So we went off to lunch at our favorite drive-in restaurant. I loved going there because all you had to do was pick up the receiver and order from the menu board. We loved having the waitress bring our food to our car window. As we finished eating, Dad suggested that we should go look at some of the Christmas decorations. It was so much fun because it was family time, and it was the holidays too.

When we arrived home, I had just enough time to change and dress before James arrived. The plan was for him to come at around five o'clock.

As I got dressed, my head spun with thoughts. *Did Mom say anything to Dad? Does Dad know what's going to happen? What if she hasn't? What will Dad say?* Dad was a big man and very stern. Once a boy stopped by to see me while Dad was cleaning his hunting gun. When Dad went to the door with the gun in his hand, the boy thought he was running him off. I never saw that boy again. We laughed about that often, but this was different. *This is the man I am going to marry just as soon as Dad gives his approval. So, what is Dad going say?* I was so nervous that I felt sick. I finished getting dressed, and James finally arrived. My sisters and brothers were sitting and waiting with much anticipation.

When James got out of his car and walked to the house, my legs turned to Jell-O as I walked to the door. I opened the door, James entered, and we all—including my Dad—just sat there looking at James and at each other. Suddenly, one of my brothers burst into laughter. That was his favorite thing to do when he got nervous. It was so funny that we all started laughing. It broke the thickest ice barrier I have ever felt in my life, and I was so glad that he had started laughing.

James sat on the couch next to my brothers and sisters, and the conversation started to flow. Dad and James started to talk about this and that. Finally, I nudged James and told him to go ahead and ask Dad.

James smiled at me and turned to look at Dad. "Ah, sir, ah, there is something I want to ask you."

Dad looked directly at James and asked, "What is it?"

"I love your daughter here, and I would like to have her hand in marriage," James said.

I sat there listening to him. I thought *James is doing so good! Everything he is saying is just what he has told me.*

My thoughts were interrupted with silence. I suddenly realized there was silence in the room, and no one was saying a word. *Oh no! What is taking Dad so long to say something? What is he going to say?* My heart was pounding so hard that I thought it would pound out of my chest. *Please say something!* Even my brother wasn't saying anything.

Finally, the silence was broken.

"As you know, James, Tawana's only sixteen years old. And I don't want you to ever hurt her. Will you promise to take care of her?" Dad asked with a slow sternness in his voice. Before James could answer, Dad went on to joke, "James, I won't give her to you, but I'll sell her to you for a nickel!"

James reached into his pocket, pulled out a nickel, and tossed it to my Dad.

I looked to Dad and asked, "Are you really saying we can get married?"

"Yes. Me and your mother are in agreement to let you and James get married."

We all started yelling, "Yes! Yes! Yes!"

Later, my Mom told me that Dad cried all that night. He kept saying that his first little girl was going to leave home with a husband. He was so sad that another man would be taking care of his little girl.

***

DECEMBER 15, 1966

During the last week of classes before Christmas school break, I told all my teachers that I wouldn't be returning after the holidays. The school counselors encouraged me to stay in school and continue my education. But with my parents' approval and being young and in love, I was sure that I all needed to do in life was to be a wife and mother.

In addition to celebrating Christmas, we were now celebrating and planning a wedding. There were so many things to do. First, we had to confirm a wedding date. James and I talked to my parents, and we decided on January 22. This date was very special to me because this was my parents' anniversary. I admired my parents and the little things that they always did for each other. My parents gave each other special cards and were always affectionate toward each other. I thought that was the way things were to be in a marriage. I'm not saying they never argued or had disagreements, because they did, but they always made up. I loved them very much, so their wedding anniversary date was a special date to me.

Our next step was to talk to our pastor and make sure the church would be available. When James and I arrived at the church where I had attended all my life, we agreed that I would ask. "James and I have approval from my parents, and we want to get married in this church and by you," I said.

"As your pastor and as your friend, let me give you some advice. Always be honest with each other, and keep the Lord in your lives. Let Him guide you," he said.

It was done.

As you can imagine, I was floating on air. I knew my parents couldn't afford a big wedding, but I didn't care just as long as I got married and became the perfect wife and mother.

DECEMBER 21, 1966

It was Friday night, and when he got home from work, James, my friend, her boyfriend, and I were going to a Christmas party. I dressed in my burgundy skirt and pink mohair sweater. James had told me that he would wear his blue velour shirt and jeans, the outfit he was wearing the very first time I met him. He told me he had a surprise for me tonight, too. We were so excited and in love.

We were all ready and waiting for James. Seven o'clock came, and James still was not there. My mind kept spinning. *Why is he not here? Where is he? The party starts at seven-thirty.* By now, it was eight o'clock, and I was worried about him. James had never done this before.

"Maybe you all should go on to the party," I suggested to my friends. "But will you drop me off at James's sister's house?" I asked. James told me that he would be staying at his sister's and would drive from there to my house.

"Sure thing," they said. And Mom thought that it was a good idea too. When I arrived at James's sister's house, I was shocked. James and his brother-in-law had decided to have a few drinks on the way home from work, to do some early celebrating. James had drunk so much that he had passed out. James's sister and her husband were packed and ready to leave on a trip to take James's mother back to her home in Kentucky. They were glad that I arrived, and they wanted me to stay and make sure James was okay, even though he probably would sleep until late in the night. I called Mom and explained things to her, and asked her if it would be okay. She agreed.

That was the first I knew of James drinking. So, with everyone gone, I picked up a book to read and waited for James to wake up. I was so upset with him. I didn't know James could do anything like this. I had never seen anyone drunk before except my grandpa—once when I was visiting my grandparents in the summer.

My dad and mom never drank or smoked. I smoked, but my parents didn't know. I planned to tell them after I got married. I guess that I thought that would mean I was my own boss and could do what I wanted.

Early in the morning, James woke up.

"What time is it?" James asked.

"It's 3 am!" I snapped.

"I am so sorry. You are going to forgive me, aren't you?" James pleaded. "I am sorry that we missed the party. I am so sorry."

I just looked at him and asked, "Are you hungry? Do you want me to fix you a sandwich?"

After we ate sandwiches, we went to the living room and sat down. Then James said, "I have a surprise for you, if you'll still marry me."

"Of course I'll still marry you," I said with a smile.

"Close your eyes and don't peak," James said in a sweet voice.

I heard James walk over to his sister's piano and raise the lid of the piano seat. "Don't look till I tell you to, okay?" James asked.

I heard James moving some papers or something. "Okay. Now you can open your eyes," he said.

James stood in front of me. He knelt down, opened a little box, and pulled out a beautiful ring. "Will you marry me?" he asked.

"YES!" I squealed. James slipped the ring on my finger. It was a perfect fit—a beautiful matching set with a band. We just sat there, holding each other. I thought, *It will be this way for us forever.* I felt so loved by him. He was so soft and gentle.

***

I almost let Christmas slip away with thoughts of what was coming my way. But once we all— including James and my sister's boyfriend—were on our way to Grandma's house for Christmas, I dropped my thoughts of me and enjoyed being with my family. It was always fun to be around my Grandma, and my sisters and I always felt we had learned a lot of 'life lessons' from her. Grandma would play the organ until we started to get sleepy, and we would just go to sleep on the floor. Things like this made going to Grandma's house so much fun.

And this visit to Grandma's was no different. It was wonderful. One game that we played was having all the men or husbands take off their shoes and hide behind a sheet, with only their feet showing. We women then tried to match the feet to the person. It was so fun. We laughed and told stories. Like the time one of my sisters thought she had eaten a goldfish, but actually it was a sardine.

We had so much fun, but we were hit with a big disappointment. Dad put our gifts in the car to keep them out of the way overnight. The next morning, the car window had been broken, and all of our gifts were gone. We were so sad, and the smaller ones cried almost all the way home. It was a very rude awakening of just what could happen in the big city. My sister's boyfriend had given her a beautiful cat, so we all enjoyed her Christmas gift.

Heading back home, I tried not to think about the lost gifts but to focus my thoughts on my wedding.

***

The holidays came and went. It was now time to focus on my wedding. There were so many things to do. Who was going to be James's best man? I decided that my sister and her boyfriend could stand up with us as our witnesses. James was fine with all the decisions that I made. Even when I talked to him about things, he seemed happy with all of my decisions.

I decided not to have a big wedding. I knew that my family couldn't afford an expensive affair, so I limited invitations to family members and few close friends. My future sister-in-law helped with so many details. We chose to have the reception at her house. She provided a beautiful blue velvet dress for my sister to wear and helped with the decision for the guys to wear gray pants and black jackets with white boutonnieres.

James bought me a dress to wear at the reception. It was a beautiful gold-sparkled dress with a black lace jacket, and I loved the way it looked on me. We decided that my sister have a bouquet of pink sweetheart roses, and I would carry pink and white roses and light-blue carnations.

JANUARY, 1967

All was done and planned—except for my wedding dress. I decided that I wanted Dad to go with me and Mom to choose a dress. When I asked him if he would, he agreed.

"Dad, would go with me today to help me pick out my wedding dress?" I asked.

"Yes, but your Mom can go with us," he said with a smile.

We went shopping to a store that had all their wedding gowns on the top floor. I had never been in a store that large. I had never seen an escalator. I wasn't expecting to see so many wedding dresses. I didn't know where to start. A sales lady saw my confusion, and she asked a few questions to help guide me. I knew that I couldn't afford anything expensive, and she helped me look through the dresses to choose a few to try on. It was so exciting!

I walked from the dressing room with the dress that I thought was 'the one.' When I walked out, Dad started to cry. We all started to cry, even the saleslady. *This is the dress. It's a perfect fit!* It was a white waltz-length dress with scallops around the neckline and cuffs of the sleeves.

Next was the veil. I found a simple and elegant veil with a single white rose and netting all around it. Now I was a little nervous about the cost of everything.

"How much will everything cost?" I asked.

"Let me ring this up for you, and we'll see," the saleslady replied.

I held my breath. "Your total is $88.00," she said.

"Eighty-eight dollars?" I yelled out. I couldn't believe that.

"The store manager said the veil is free because it's the last one."

Everything seemed to be working out for me. Driving home, my parents and I just kept saying how the good Lord had blessed us.

This was 1967. Things were different back then—everything was.

Our families got together the Friday night before the wedding. They were so excited and happy to hear about the little house that James and I had rented.

James and I found a small house with three rooms and a bath. We purchased all new furniture. I had a hope chest with things people had given to me, and I had quite a few things saved up to go in my little house. The little house was so cute. James and I had to go to the grocery store and purchase everything from sugar to bologna. We spent $44.00, which does not sound like much today, but when your monthly rent is only $40.00, it puts a different perspective on things.

JANUARY 21, 1967

The big day is tomorrow. I had a wonderful evening with Mom, Dad, and my brothers and sisters talking about my future. I realized just how much I loved my entire family. They were very special to me and it was important to them for me to have a special wedding. I was so excited that I could not sleep, and I just kept thinking about I was getting married to my Prince Charming and that I was going to be the perfect wife and mother.

CHAPTER 3

JANUARY 22, 1967
WEDDING DAY

I was so excited! I could hardly believe that this was the day that I had waited for so long. The wedding was scheduled for 2 pm. We packed the car and headed to the church. My wedding dress was in the back with me and my two sisters. My two brothers sat up front with Mom and Dad. We looked like sardines packed in a can.

We made it to the church. I was getting so nervous that I was worried that I wouldn't be able to walk down the aisle. James's family, my family, and our friends began to arrive at the church. It was good to know that they are there and wanted to be a part of this special day for us.

My sister looked so beautiful in her blue velvet dress. Mom had a lovely sweater suit, and Dad wore his black suit. My other sister had a pretty dress to wear, and my brothers had nice little suits.

By 1:30 pm, I was fully dressed. I realized that no one had mentioned that James had arrived. *Will he stand me up on my wedding day? What will I do?*

I asked Dad if he would go check to see if James had arrived. I was thankful to hear that James was there—he was just running late.

The music started to play. It was time. Mom walked down the aisle, then my sister, and soon it was time for me to walk down the aisle. I looked to Dad, and he started to cry. I whispered to him not to cry because if he did, I would. He tried to smile, and we started walking down the aisle.

I could see my sister and her boyfriend, who was the best man, and James standing there with the pastor. It seemed so far down that aisle to James.

"Who gives this bride in marriage?" the preacher asked.

"Her Mother and I do," answered Dad.

James took my hand, and I looked him in the eyes. He looked at me in the eyes, and suddenly I felt that no one was in the church except the preacher, James, and me. We exchanged vows and the preacher said, "I now present to you all James and Tawana Campbell as husband and wife."

We turned around and started our life together.

All of the family members were going to my sister-in-law's house for cake and punch. We were so excited that we blew the car horn so much that it got stuck on our way to their house. *Wow, I am actually Mrs. Tawana Campbell.* I had practiced writing it so many times, but now it was true.

We arrived at my sister-in-law's house, and I changed into the pretty dress that James had given to me for Christmas. Everyone was so happy for us. We sat and talked to everyone. I was told that I was a lovely bride. I felt so beautiful on my wedding day. *Isn't this how all brides should feel on their wedding day?*

By 8:30 pm, our guests began to leave, so James and I decided to leave too. Tonight we would leave as husband and wife. We rode around town for a short time and then headed to our little home. We had worked so hard to make the house look cute. I had it just the way I wanted it. When we arrived home, we were ready to jump in bed. To our surprise, we found crackers in our bed. Yes, crackers! It was so funny, but at the time, we could not figure out who put them there. No one had a key, but later we found out that it was my Mom and Dad. That is one of those things you always remember. That is what makes memories.

We didn't have a real honeymoon until James' vacation during the summer, so he had to go to work the next morning. That morning was a wonderful January day—the sun was shining brightly, and snow was on the ground. James was off to work, and I finished getting the remaining crackers out of the bedroom and worked around *our* house.

I knew that James would come home to me after work. I prepared supper to be ready by the time he got home. This was all I wanted. I was so happy. I knew that I could be a good housewife and mother. This was going to be everything I had dreamed it would be. Taking care of the house, doing household chores—all the while, James would be working and taking care of me. Things were going to be so good. I visualized how my family would come to visit us, eat supper with us, and enjoy my cooking. Mom and Dad had been my teachers, so I believed I was a good cook. This was sort of like playing house to me—I cleaned, cooked, did laundry, and was going to be a very good wife to my husband.

SIX WEEKS LATER

Things changed quickly, especially with James. He came home late every evening. By the time he arrived home, I was crying from worry and from wondering where he might be. Here I was. I wasn't old enough to get my driver's license—at that time, you had to be eighteen years old. I couldn't drive, and I didn't have a car. Each time James came home late, it caused an argument.

"Where have you been?" I screamed. "I have been sick with worry."

"Why don't you just take care of yourself, and I can take care of myself?" he barked.

"What is wrong with you?" I asked. "What has changed?"

"Nothing!"

It was always the same. I just could not figure out what had happened to him. I was doing what I thought he wanted. I was staying home and trying to be the good wife. For some reason, it did not seem to be enough for him, because it seemed that I was doing nothing right for him.

Next to come were the accusations. "What have you done all day? You've been sneaking out with your friends, haven't you?"

"No! My friends don't come over anymore because I'm married!" I yelled.

It seemed hopeless. Things were not getting better. He wouldn't talk to me, much less listen to me. He was convinced that all his accusations were true even though they were just in his imagination.

It was serious. It was not getting better. I decided that I was going to leave him.

"I cannot take this any longer! I am leaving! I am going back home!"

I decided to go back home for the weekend to think about what I was going to do in this situation. I knew I loved James and wanted to be his wife. I was so confused and could not understand this part of our life.

I got in touch with Mom. "Mom, I'd like to visit you and the kids this weekend. Can you come and get me?" I asked.

"Sure. We miss you and would love to see you," she replied.

As soon as I saw them, I couldn't believe how much I had missed everyone. As soon as Mom saw me, she recognized that I had been crying.

"Tawana, what's the matter?" Mom asked.

When Mom asked, I just broke down crying.

"What has he done to you?" Mom demanded.

"Mom, I don't know where to start," I said. "He never comes home until real late; he won't talk to me and just tells me that it is none of my business. Mom, he accuses me of going places with people and of having people over to the house," I said. "Mom, I can't even drive, and I don't have a car!"

Mom listened to me. It was good to be with my family. We spend time together, doing things together, but I was miserable without James. I cried the whole weekend.

Late Sunday evening, James showed up. He knocked on the door and asked if I would talk to him. When I got to the door and James saw me, he quickly said,

"I am so sorry. Please come back home. I am very sorry. Will you please come back home?"

I had been so miserable all weekend without him, and I could not imagine my life without him, so I answered, "Yes."

***

It started over again, but this time I was serious. I had decided I was leaving, and I started to pack everything. I mean everything—I even took the curtains off the windows. I was hurt and angry; I had worked hard on *our* house and I was not going to leave a thing; and I was going to leave the house bare.

This time, James seemed happy that I was leaving. He helped me to pack and to put all my things in the car. He agreed that he would drive me to my parents' house.

When we arrived, Dad was already home from his week's work. We parked the car in the driveway, James grabbed a lamp out of the car, and I loaded my arms with as many things as I could carry. We walked to the door.

Dad opened the door and asked, "What is going on here?"

"She wants to come back home. We're not getting along," James snapped.

I was so relieved that I was finally home—around family and people that I loved and loved me.

"Now, you just take her and yourself back to your home where you belong. You both wanted to get married and be together. You sure can't run back here every time you think something goes wrong. You get her in that car and don't bring her back!" Dad announced. "Do you hear me? This is the bed you made, you lay in it."

I froze in my steps. *Oh no! If I can't come back to Mom's and Dad's house, where can I go?* Reality hit me full in the face. I had nowhere to go but back with James.

We carried the things back to the car. We drove back without speaking a word. I knew I didn't want to go back home with James, but I had no choice. After we had carried everything inside the house, James looked at me and said, "Well, now what are you going to do? Even your Dad won't let you go back home."

That night I cried myself to sleep. *What am I going to do?* On that day, I think I started on a downhill slide into depression. None of this made sense to me. *Is this actually something I did? I can't think of anything I've done to deserve what is happening to me. Why is the only thing I ever wanted falling apart?*

James went to work the next morning. I found out later that Mom and Dad came over to check on me—I was okay physically, but I was a mess emotionally. My Dad had stood outside the house and listened to see if he could hear us fighting. When he didn't hear anything, he and Mom went back home. Mom told later that when Dad told me that I could not come back home, it was the hardest thing he had ever done in his life. Dad knew that if he had allowed his 'little girl' to come back home, he knew things would never work out between James and me.

I never, ever told James again that I wanted to leave.

APRIL 1967

James and I had begun to communicate better; we had fewer arguments, and we even shared laughter again. By this time, James had started to talk about going back to New Jersey. This bothered me. I didn't want to go somewhere with no friends and family, and James had promised that he wouldn't take me far away from home. But the promise didn't change things, and before I knew what was happening, we were putting our furniture in storage and packing everything into the car that we could. So, with just the basics in the car, we made our rounds telling everyone goodbye. I did have one request, though. I had such a fear of living far away and was so uncomfortable about leaving that I asked James to take me to see my parents. I had this strange feeling that I might never see them again.

***

We planned to visit James's parents on the way to New Jersey. This meant that our trip would take us through eastern Kentucky. I had never been out of the state of Indiana except to visit my grandparents, who were over the bridge and south of Louisville. But now I was going to the eastern part of Kentucky—to the mountains and the coal mines—and this scared me.

It was late at night, and I was so nervous that I was smoking one cigarette after another. We were driving through a small town when suddenly we heard a siren and saw red lights flashing. There were two cars. I thought my heart was going to explode inside of my chest.

"Put this somewhere," James said as he handed all the money we had on us to pay for our trip to New Jersey. I took some of my cigarettes from the pack, rolled up the money, stuck it into the pack, and stuffed the pack in my blouse. I did all of this as we were pulled to the side of the road and stopped. My hands were shaking. I saw a fear on James face that I had never seen before.

"No matter what happens, you do what I tell you," James commanded. That scared me even more. I thought, *Jesus is our only hope.* I started to pray for Jesus to help to us.

The next thing I knew, a big man with a badge was standing at the car door. He asked James for his driver's license. James handed it to him. The officer looked at the license and then shined his flashlight into the back seat, which was full of all our things.

"Where are you going?" the officer asked.

"To my parents," James answered.

The officer kept shinning his flashlight around the car, and he kept looking at all our stuff packed in the back seat.

When he handed James's license back to him, the officer said, "You need to come into town and pay a fine for speeding."

"Yes sir," James said.

It was 11 pm, and we didn't see a sign for a town. We pulled behind the squad cars. We followed them through town and saw that nothing was open. We drove by what we thought was the city hall or police station, but we continued until we were on the other side of town.

"I think they're going to rob us," James said. I almost fainted. My heart was pounding!

As the front car slowed down, James said, "We need to let them think that we are going to go with them until I see away of out of this and get away from them. We can't do anything rash, 'cause they have our license plate number and can find us."

The front car put on its left turn signal, and James put his on, too. We slowed down enough so that we could see we were still on a blacktop road, but once we turned, we would be traveling down into a holler. We saw by the front car's headlights that this was a backwoods road, and there were a lot of little houses on blocks and wooden stilts. I had never seen houses like that before.

Just as it looked like James was going to follow and turn down this road, he yelled, "Hold on tight! We're getting out of here!" He rammed the car in reverse, just missing the back car, and whipped the car around. He put the car in drive and drove like a mad man. We hit 80 miles per hour.

We were frightened nearly to death. We knew if they caught us, they would probably kill us. We were strangers, and no one would ever know what had happened to us if we disappeared. Finally, we reached the out-skirts of town. I am sure that the hand of God directed us and led us to a place made just for our car. There was a service station on the main road. We turned into the station and saw that in the back, there was a rock wall and just enough room to pull our car in the space behind the station and that rock wall.

Having never been in the town before, I believe that it was the hand of God that guided us to that spot. We slipped into that spot like slipping on a glove. We heard a car speed by, so we figured it was probably them. We continue to sit for what seemed like hours.

Finally James started the car and backed out slowly as he looked for any lights. We turned onto the main road and away we went, as fast as we could go. We were still about an hour and half from Hazard, Kentucky. James seemed to know some of the back roads, and being a Hoosier from the flat land of Indiana, I had never seen elbow curves. It was obvious that we were getting farther and farther away from town and deeper into the mountains.

The further we went, the more curves encountered. James was sitting almost halfway in the middle of the seat on some of these curves. Suddenly, we were on road with nothing except a mountain and the side of a cliff, and we are rounding an S curve.

"Hold on tight as you can!" James yelled. "It helps to hold onto me." As we rounded, he was almost sitting in my lap, holding on to the steering wheel and trying to keep his feet on the gas pedal at the same time.

"I can't do this anymore! I don't want to do this!" I screamed.

"Shut up!" he said. "I'll take care of you. You just don't need to be screaming."

"But I want to be anywhere but here! I am scared to death!" I yelled back. "How much further is it?"

"We are about 15 miles away. That's all," James said.

"Thank goodness!" I snapped.

Shortly, we turned onto a one-lane side road. There was a river on one side and a railroad on the other side of us. This was the most unusual place in the world to me.

"We're here," James said.

"Finally! Uh, where is the house?" I asked.

"Up this holler," James said and started to laugh. James turned the car into what he called the 'head of the holler.' It was pitch black. You couldn't see anything except what the headlights showed. He shifted the car down into a lower gear to climb up this hill.

I started to cry. I was scared out of my mind. I was only sixteen and had never been away from home—and now this! It seemed that the car was going roll over backward before we arrived at the house.

Suddenly, through my tears, I saw lights coming in view, and it looked like there was a house on a hillside. I was so happy I could see something besides black midnight. I just couldn't wait to get out of the car, but I was unsure if my feet and legs would allow me to stand. I felt wobbly. It was 2:00 in the morning.

We had to walk to the house from the flat spot where we parked the car. James was used to this, but I wasn't. By the time we got to the porch, my legs were like jelly. Immediately inside, we were in a kitchen, and I sat down. I tried to get myself and my thoughts together.

This was the very first time I had met some of James's relatives, like his other brothers and sisters. We quickly went to bed since we both were so exhausted. I thought, *Surely things will look better in the daylight. My world had changed so much so fast!*

I was awakened suddenly. It had to be early in the morning.

"James, I heard something. What time is it?" I asked.

"Get your breakfast! Hurry! Get up and eat before its get cold," someone yelled from the kitchen.

"James, wake up. What time is it?" I asked.

"It looks like it's about 5 am," James answered.

"Why are we supposed to get up so early?" I asked.

"Mom always gets up around 4:30 or 5 am to get breakfast ready for everyone. That includes us. So we better get up," James said.

I just wanted to stay in bed, but on the other hand, I wanted to see this place. This was the place that my husband called 'the home place'—Perry County, Kentucky. I had never heard of it. It was very small, and this area was called Campbell's Creek.

At daybreak, when I stepped onto the porch, all I could see was the side of a mountain. When I walked around the side of the house, I saw a giant rock in the edge of the yard. I was shocked. The biggest shocker was when James pointed out where the outside toilet was setting. It sat right on the edge of the creek and had tall weeds all around it. All I could think about was snakes.

I was nervous about us staying and not leaving for New Jersey until Sunday morning. But his relatives were curious about me and what it was like to live in Indiana. I was curious about them as well. I shared with them that I was born in a small town—Beech Grove, Indiana—and was raised in a smaller town called Austin, where a big canning factory was located.

It was interesting to learn about James's siblings and their families. Their Dad worked in the coal mines until he was laid off. Their Mom always worked around the house—cooking, cleaning, and sewing. She made all of their clothes. She never used a pattern, and she used a pedal Singer sewing machine. They shared with me that they could shop in town only on Saturday mornings, and they went by bus.

I really enjoyed my visit with James's family. I liked them, and they seemed to like me too. My hope was that we all would be friends.

It was early Sunday morning when I heard James's mom in the kitchen. Not only did I hear her, but I smelled the best aroma ever.

"It's time to get up! Get your breakfast before it gets cold!" she yelled.

James and I headed to the kitchen. We knew that we would have a long ride ahead of us, going to New Jersey, so we did not mind getting up early. As we walked into the kitchen, I couldn't believe all the food she had cooked for breakfast. She had prepared fried eggs—with soft and hard yolks—and scrambled eggs. She had prepared sausage, bacon, and fried chicken. I was amazed! I thought, *Fried chicken for breakfast? We have it for Sunday dinner!* Of course, she had prepared homemade biscuits and brown gravy, and both were the best I had ever eaten.

We ate, helped clean up, and packed the car. We walked to the car, said our good-byes to everyone, and were on our way again. I knew that the rest of the trip would be better. It was! We saw beautiful landscapes along the east coast. We travelled through the mountains of Virginia and the Shenandoah Valley. It was beautiful.

CHAPTER 4

We arrived at James's brother's house in Vineland, New Jersey, and they were expecting us. We got a few things from the car and settled in for the night to get some rest. James was to start work the next morning at the same company where he worked before he came to Indiana on vacation.

***

After 2 weeks, I still didn't know anyone. I felt so alone and so lost. My brother and sister- in -law were very nice to me and allowed us to stay there until were got a place of our own. We found a small apartment in a small town close to James's work. We were on the top floor of the building, and we had no stove or refrigerator, so James picked up something for supper for us as on his way home. We used a hot plate and an electric skillet to cook our food.

When James went to work, I straightened up the apartment and listened to a little transistor radio that a friend had given to me when I quit school. I listened to it all day, and I played Solitaire until I wore the color off the backs of the cards. I found myself eating snack foods. That was basically all we had to eat.

James worked every day and was gone all day. I definitely was not going to go outside because I was too scared. That fear seemed to increase each day. I didn't want to feel scared all the time, but I did.

After another two weeks, we tried to locate to a trailer court that was within walking distance from James's employment. We found one, so we were in the apartment approximately three weeks.

Moving day arrived. Another move, but I look forward to this move because we were moving into town. The trailer we moved into needed a lot of cleaning. I scrubbed till it was shining. I was so proud of it and my hard work. Now, if we had visitors or guests, my house looked good. It was such a good feeling that when James and I went to the grocery store, I actually had a place to put my groceries and cook food. I purchased food that I could actually prepare on my stove, which even had a griddle. I cooked soup beans, baked cornbread, and prepared homemade biscuits and gravy. Things were good. Sometimes after work, James would stop and pick up my favorite steak sub sandwich.

We were still settling into our new home after a couple of weeks, when I meet a young woman in the next trailer. When she saw me outside, she started up a conversation, and we became friends. Sometimes I invited her over to visit during the day when James was at work. She never invited me over to her house, though; she only came my place to visit.

One day, she and I were talking about everyday things when she said, "James and some of his friends and his brother all used to live in this trailer court. Did you know that?"

I was shocked. I never really let on, but James had never told me. I thought that as soon as James came home, I would ask him.

After James had arrived home and we had settled in for the evening, I asked, "James, have you lived in this trailer court before?"

He immediately became upset. "Where did you hear that? Your new friend next door? I don't want you talking to her anymore! She just made that up! Do not talk to her anymore! Do you understand me?" he asked.

I was surprised at James's reaction, so I had to believe that maybe she was wrong. After James went to work the next day, I saw her outside.

"James said that saying that he had lived here was untrue," I said in a kind tone.

"Honey," she replied, "I'm not making anything up. I know him. I have seen him before."

I was confused. I wanted to believe her, but I wanted to believe James. I decided that I would still talk to her, but that I wouldn't bring it up with James.

***

Each move meant more expenses for us. We were running short on money, and I still had my habit of smoking cigarettes. When I was out of cigarettes, I gathered soda bottles and took them to the store. At that time, people could trade the bottles for money. That's was the way I got my cigarettes.

I received a letter from my Mom and Dad. They wanted to come up and see us sometime in May. I was so excited! My family would be coming all that way to see us! I just couldn't wait! It seemed like such a long time since I had seen them. I was so young and scared and felt so lost without the comfort of my family. I replied,

Hi, Mom and Dad!

I can't wait to see you!

I have not seen you all since March, and here it is the first of May! When will you be here?

Mom wrote back that they would arrive around the end of May or the first of June. Perfect timing! I was hoping that maybe one of my sisters could stay the summer with me. With James's uncle and aunt living up here too, we could visit their little farm. We would have fun picking vegetables and the biggest red strawberries around, called Jersey Bells.

James and I decided to visit his uncle's farm to pick strawberries to sell along the roadside. This would provide us a little extra money for my family's visit.

James and I picked crates of berries and took them to the main road into Atlantic City, where his brother lived. It was a good idea in theory, but all weekend, we did not sell one berry. We couldn't even give them away. *What is wrong with these people?!* I could have sold all these berries in an hour back home in Indiana. It was a reality check. I definitely was not in Indiana, and I started feeling homesick.

Knowing that my family would appreciate the strawberries, James and I picked two more crates of fresh berries just for their visit. I stored the berries in the bottom of the fridge so they wouldn't dry out. I knew that my family would arrive the next day, and it would be exciting to share these beautiful berries with them.

At 9:30 pm, I started to walk the floor and watch the clock in anticipation of their arrival. I figured that they would arrive late in the evening.

"You know a watched pot never boils," James said.

"But it's 11 o'clock, and they're not here yet. Do you think they may have had car trouble or stopped because of one of the kids or something?" I asked James.

"Well, why don't you lie down? You know how it is when you are waiting for someone. And you can hear a car pull up," James said.

I did lie down and must have dropped off to sleep. When I woke up, it was morning and daylight. They were not here. I was frantic.

"Maybe they went ahead and stopped at a motel since it got late," James said.

"Sure. I bet that was what they did," I replied, feeling disappointed.

"What if they decided not to come?" James asked.

What if they had decided not to come? They had no way of getting hold of us. What if something had happened to them—like what happened to James and me?

I waited and waited all day, with my hope of seeing family fading with each passing hour. They never showed. I cried all afternoon and all night.

All those berries! I was sick of them. I gave them all to the girl next door.

I really needed to see my family and to talk to them. I needed to feel their presence near me. This was just another disappointment in my life. Things between James and me were getting bad again, and I just needed to feel their love for me.

With each disappointment, I felt more out of control. My weight a couple months ago was 135 pounds, but now had I gained 15 or 20 pounds. *What if—can I be pregnant?* I thought that would be wonderful! I wanted to have a baby since James and I had gotten married. I knew that I could be the best wife and mother. But within a short time, I found that I was not pregnant. Just another disappointment for me. But I decided that it was probably for the best since James and I were not getting along very well.

James had started to stay out late after work, and it was obvious that he was drinking.

"Where have you been?" I asked.

"It's none of your business!" James snapped. "I can take care of myself!"

It was always the same questions, with same answers. One evening, I asked him to replace a light bulb in the bathroom and to fix it. He just seemed to ignore me. I decided that I would repair it myself.

The next day, while James was at work, there was a knock at the door in the early morning. I was still in my bedclothes—a gown and robe—but I answered the door.

"I am the maintenance man, and I was checking to see if there is anything that I can fix for you," he said.

At that same moment, James drove up. I stood in the doorway talking to the man for no more than a couple of minutes, telling him that everything was okay and that we didn't need anything fixed. I saw a look in James's eyes. James was suspicious. James spoke to the man. They talked for a few minutes, and the man left.

James came inside. "Who was that man?" he asked.

"He said that he was the maintenance guy here," I answered.

"And why are you still in your night clothes?" James asked harshly.

"He knocked on the door, and I just answered it," I said defensively.

I turned from the conversation and went to get dressed. It was just easier to stay in my gown and robe. None of my clothes fit anymore. Whenever I asked James for new clothes, he was always quick to tell me that we didn't have any money to buy clothes and that we had to pay our bills first. It seemed we never had any money any more. I traded in pop bottles to buy cigarettes, but I didn't have enough to buy clothes.

Here it was, early to mid-morning, and James was home. I was so surprised.

"Why are you home so early?" I asked.

"They ran out of work," James said.

"I'll fix some lunch for you," I said.

"I'm not hungry," James said.

"Okay," I said, "I'm not very hungry either."

James walked outside and piddled around all afternoon. It was near dinnertime, and I started to prepare food, when James came inside and walked to the bathroom.

James walked into the bathroom, switched on the light, and it worked. "How did this light get fixed?" James asked sharply.

"I fixed it, "I answered. "I fixed it this morning. All I had to do was replace it with a new bulb. I took a bulb out of the lamp that we aren't using."

"You had that man inside this house, didn't you?" James yelled at me. War between us was on again.

"That man was in here! He fixed it didn't he?" James screamed at me. "No!" I yelled. "I did it myself! He was not in here!"

Without warning, James picked up my what-nots and started breaking them into little pieces.

"Stop it! Stop it!" How could you do this? You son of bitch!" I screamed.

My world came to an alarming halt. I was hit.

James hit me. Did I deserve this for calling him a name?

I was numb. But my tears came rushing like a raging flood. *What is going on with us?*

James walked out the door, slamming it behind him. He got in the car and left. *Where is he going? What does he do for hours?* I had no idea. Again, I felt an overcoming fear. I was alone, I had no one turn to, and I was scared. I started to pray. *God, please let me get back to Indiana. Please God. Provide a way for me to get back to Indiana to my mom. God, I want to start going back to church. If you will just let me get back home, I will start going to church. Amen.*

By ten o'clock, James was still not home. I tried to clean up the mess he had made by breaking all my things. The pieces were everywhere. All my special things were broken.

James finally showed up at about midnight. When he walked inside, it was clear that he had been drinking. As soon as he walked through the door, he started again with accusations.

"You've had men in here, haven't you? Just admit it, 'cause I know that you have!" James said, with the alcohol slurring his words.

He started throwing things again. He broke my lamp and grabbed my little transistor radio. I tried to take it back from him but couldn't. He smashed it on the floor and then stomped on it.

I was devastated! *What is wrong with him?* I didn't understand.

I ran to the bedroom, got in bed, and covered my head. I couldn't bear it any longer. As I lay there crying, I could still hear him breaking things. He walked into the bedroom as I was crying and hollered more accusations.

"Shut up! Leave me alone!" I cried.

James sat down on the bed and said, "You are no good! You are a bad girl! Nobody cares about you! Did you know that? Nobody! Not even your family!"

James moves from the side of the bed to sitting on top of me. He grabbed my hair, and yelled, "You are a whore! You are a filthy whore!"

Somewhere between his cursing me and calling me all kinds of awful names, I passed out. I must have gone into shock. The next thing I remember, I was waking up in the hospital emergency room, with a nurse standing over me, asking "Honey, can you hear me? Honey. Honey, can you open your eyes?"

I opened my eyes. I saw James standing outside the room.

"Can I see James?" I asked.

"Only for a few minutes," the nurse said.

The nurse stepped outside the room, and James walked over to me. He leaned over and said, "Don't let them call the police on me. If you do, the police will put me in jail."

"I want to go home. Will you put me on the first bus out of here?" I asked quietly.

"We don't have the money to buy a ticket. I will have to get the money from someone. You are not staying another night in Jersey." James said.

Still standing over me, James said, "You do not tell them what happened to you. If you do, I will have to go to jail. And I know that you don't want that to happen because you want me to get you back home."

The nurse came back and said, "You have to step back outside, sir."

James walked out of the room looking back at me with hardness in his eyes. "Now, honey, I have some questions for you. Can you tell me what happened to you?" asked the nurse.

"I really don't remember what actually happened to me. We had been arguing, but I don't remember anything else," I answered.

"Are you sure, honey?" the nurse asked.

"I'm sure," I said.

"Now, are you sure?" the nurse asked again.

"Yes, I am sure," I replied.

This went on for a few minutes, but then the nurse asked, "Do you have anyone you want us to call for you?"

Oh, how I wanted to say yes, but I said, "No. There is no one."

After a long wait, the doctor came in and said, "You have had a nervous breakdown. You are very young woman to be experiencing this sort of thing."

I just looked at him. I wanted to scream and cry, but I just stared at him.

"How long have you been married?" he asked.

"About five months," I replied.

"Are you happy?" he asked in a monotone.

I fought back tears and said, "Yes."

"I can have your husband put in jail for doing this to you," he said in that monotone again.

"Oh no! Please no! I beg of you! Please do not do that," I pleaded. I just wanted to go home. I wanted James with me.

As the doctor wrote a prescription for some medicine he said, "Take care of yourself. You are a very lucky young lady. Some people don't come out of breakdowns, and sometimes they never get over them." To this day, I still have no idea how long I was out before I got to the hospital or how I actually got to the hospital.

I truly believed that I was lucky.

On our way home, James promised that he would treat me better. He vowed that if I would wait, he and I would move back to Indiana on the Fourth of July weekend. He promised. I promised him that if he did not treat me better, I was going to leave on that bus.

***

A few weeks later, I saw on a flyer in the store that the Barnum and Bailey Circus was coming to town. I suggested to James that we go to the circus. He agreed. When the circus arrived in town, their set-up was only a mile or so from our house. I could see the top of the big tent from our door. I was so excited. But our Saturday morning walk to the circus was just to walk, talk, and look. We didn't have enough money to buy admission tickets. I had to tell myself that someday I would be able to go to the big-top circus.

It was the last week of June, and I was getting things ready for the move. It was not going to take me long to pack our things because most of my what-nots were gone. I went to the local Goodwill and found a couple of outfits to wear home. I was able to trade some of my clothes that I couldn't wear any more for ones that I could wear. I wrote to Mom and told her that we were coming home the next weekend and that I was excited to see them. I did not tell her about anything that had happened to me or with James and me. I did not see a need to worry her. Besides, she wouldn't be able to do anything except worry.

It was time. Finally! The worst three months of my life were going to be over. The day before, we had said all our goodbyes to James's brothers and to my friend next door.

We were packed and in the car when James said, "We are going to pick up a friend of mine."

I was unsure where this friend, who James hadn't told me about, was going to sit in the car. But we picked him up, and his stuff went in the back of seat with our stuff. The three of us sat up front. I was in the middle. I sure didn't want to touch this guy in any way shape or form for fear of what James might think. But, on the other hand, it was James's fault for putting me in this situation.

We only made quick stops to get gas, go to the bathroom, and get a bite to eat. We arrived late at night, and by the time we arrived in Hazard, Kentucky, I needed to get out of the car. My feet and legs were swollen so badly that I could hardly stand on them to walk to the house. Everyone just sort of looked at me, and someone yelled, "Boy, it must be agreeing with you." I knew what they were thinking. Everyone thought that I was pregnant. But I knew that I wasn't.

The stay over was a quick one, but James said that he wanted to do something on Sunday, so it would Monday before we would be on the road again. For comfort, James's mom located a pair of maternity pants and a top for me to wear.

It was noon on Monday before we got on the road again. We were just a few hours from home. I could not wait to see Mom and Dad.

We finally arrived! When we pulled in front of my house, Mom, and my brothers and sisters were sitting in front of the house. I got out of the car, and everyone sat there. I looked at them and they looked at me.

Finally I said, "It's me—Tawana. It's me!"

Suddenly, they all came running and crying. "You've changed so much we didn't recognize you!"

Mom just looked at my clothes and at me. She never said a word about it. It was almost like I was a stranger in my own home. But I was so glad to be there, it didn't matter to me what they thought. They would all know soon enough anyway. It was the Fourth of July weekend, and I was not going to spoil it for anyone.

I had not shared with anyone the problems that James and I had had in New Jersey, because I truly did love him, and I didn't want anyone to think badly of him. What was the point in telling anyone? So I didn't. I decided I wouldn't tell. It would be my secret.

During the weekend, everyone came over, and I was so excited to see them all. I hadn't seen any one since we had left on our trip, so I was really glad to be home and be a part of this wonderful weekend. My Dad had always had a big fireworks display. We never knew what to expect, but always knew we would have a wonderful Fourth of July.

It was such a wonderful day, and by afternoon, we began preparations for homemade ice cream. We all took turns in turning the handle, and very soon we had delicious homemade ice cream. Mom, Grandma, my aunt, and I were all in kitchen cleaning and getting things together, when my Grandma asked, "What's the matter with you?"

"Nothing. Why do you ask that?" I asked.

"I can just tell there is something wrong with you. I can sense these things sometimes. And I know there's something wrong. I just can't put my finger on it right now," Grandma said. "If that James ever hurts you in any way, I'll take a butcher knife to him. Do you hear?"

I knew that Grandma would do exactly what she said. I just kept silent. But I knew deep down in my heart that Grandma and Mom realized that there was a problem.

As the day ended with spectacular fireworks, my grandparents and everyone had to leave to go home. It was getting late, and it took an hour and a half to drive home. My Grandpa needed to get up early to milk the cows, so they had to leave and go on their way. We were all tired and ready to go to bed.

CHAPTER 5

First thing in the morning, Mom and I scanned the local newspaper for houses for rent. We arranged to see three different properties. James had gone back to work at the factory where he had worked previously, so as soon as he got home, we went to look at the rentals. We liked the first one so much that we rented it immediately.

James knew that while he was at work, Mom and I would clean the house and get things ready so that we could move in as soon as possible. Still not eighteen years old, I couldn't get my driver's license, and I had to depend on someone else for my transportation. I was old enough to marry—but nothing else.

The next morning, after the kids were off to school, Mom and I went to the little house and started cleaning. By afternoon, we had the house in move-in condition for James and me. So, when James got home from work, his brother, a couple of his friends, and my sister's boyfriend helped us move into the house. We had some furniture that we had stored at his relatives, and it was brought to the house.

It was great! Mom and I picked up lunchmeat, cheese, soft drinks, and chips so that we could prepare sandwiches for everyone. We unpacked things and arranged furniture. I was excited that I had an extra bedroom for anytime the kids wanted to stay over.

It was late when everyone left. It was like being in a new home for James and me. It was almost like our wedding night. It was romantic, warm, and cozy. I thought, *Maybe we'll make it after all.* I loved James very much, and I desperately wanted our marriage to work. As I lay in bed, I fell asleep recalling the preacher' words, "I tied a double knot with you two."

The next morning, James and I were up together, and then he was out the door to work. I sat down and looked at what James had made possible for me. *I have a lovely home with beautiful things, and I really am blessed in so many ways.* I knew things were going to be different now. *They really can't get much worse, can they?*

All of this occurred during our first six months of marriage. I determined to make it all work. Our house was about four miles from Mom and Dad. We lived about as close to a restaurant that was the place to be on Friday and Saturday nights, and we were close enough to walk to it. With school out, we could have relatives stay over and have real family connections.

MAY 1968

It had been almost a year since we had moved back, and James was now working a new job. Things were going fairly smoothly when we received some tragic news. One of James's sisters took her own life. She left behind three little boys. James was close to his sister, and he was shaken by her passing. His mom was devastated. She cried and hit herself on her legs until they were black and blue. She was a wreck.

It was decided to bring James's sister's body to his Mom's house for the memorial service. I had never been around a funeral like this before. My family always had services at a funeral home, so this type of service was something I would never forget. The casket was placed in the front room of James's mom's house. Everyone came by there to show their love and respect for his sister.

***

By the end of June, we moved again—this time into a house that was for sale. Once it sold, we'd be moving again. It seemed like all we did was pack and unpack and pack up again. We lived in Austin, where the canning factory was located and which was seasonally busy. Every year, Mom went to work there during the canning season. But this year, as the season started, Mom suggested that I go to work there.

"Why don't you get a job at the canning factory this summer?" Mom asked. "Would you like to do that?"

"Mom, I would love to," I answered, "but I will have to discuss it with James."

I was excited at the thought of having a job.

As soon as James came home from work, I told him about Mom's idea.

"Do you think that it would be okay for me to work there for a while? Just to see if I like it?" I asked.

"You don't have to work," James said. "I can take care of you."

My heart sank, but I wanted to do this. "I know that I don't have to work. I just thought I might do it for a while. Do you think it'll be okay?" I asked.

"I guess so," James answered.

There was a lot of paperwork that I had to complete because I was only seventeen years old. I didn't have a Social Security Number or a worker's permit. It was August before I actually started working, and by September, we were moving again. The house sold, so with my job on day shift, James working night shift, and moving, I was truly experiencing the role of a wife and homemaker. Mom picked me up to take me to work. It was challenging, but I liked it.

***

James's dad visited often, and we were very comfortable with his visits. I had wonderful in-laws. One day, James went squirrel hunting and killed a squirrel. His dad offered to come over to cook squirrel dinner for us. When I got home that afternoon, I went into the kitchen and saw a pot on the stove. I lifted the lid, looked inside, and saw the full body of a squirrel curled around the cooker.

I screamed, "What is this in this cooker?"

His Dad came running into the kitchen, "Tawana, I went ahead and fixed this for us for supper."

"But why didn't you cut the head off?" I questioned.

Through loud laughter, he said, "I always leave the head on 'em when I fix a squirrel."

"Why?" I asked.

"Because I crack open the head and eat the brains," he replied very seriously.

By this time, my head was spinning, and I was in a real tizzy.

"Please! Don't leave anything like that on my stove again!" I commanded.

Later, it became a joke between us. James's dad would tease me about 'fixin' squirrel for me.

***

Thanksgiving was at Mom and Dad's, and all went well. It was now close to Christmas, and with my work, I had my own spending money. I could buy a Christmas gift for James with my own money. I always had felt funny about buying him a gift with his own money.

Since Thanksgiving was at my parents, I wanted to have Christmas at our house. Everyone agreed. James and I were getting along much better, and I looked forward to decorating my house and celebrating the holiday with my family in my house.

We had a wonderful holiday—even after losing my money when I went shopping with Mom and Dad. I went to pay for my things, but when I reached into my pocket, my $20.00 was gone. I began to cry. Dad comforted me and paid for my things. He told me that I could pay him back. I told James what happened, and he said that I should have been more careful. I was careful, but I didn't want this to damper the festive mood, so I put it out of my mind. We had a wonderful holiday.

***

JANUARY 22, 1969

This was our second anniversary. I thought that it seemed like it had been forever. I had started to go to church some with Mom and Dad and the kids. I could only get there by having them stop by and take me with them. James wouldn't go with me. I wanted him to, but he didn't.

On James's birthday, he turned twenty-five. I had finally turned eighteen and believed that we were going to make it. Our next holiday was Easter. I thought it was a perfect time for James to start attending church with me.

"James, Mom, Dad, and I are planning to attend service. Would you like to go with us?"

"No, I don't think so," James answered.

"Why not?" I asked.

"'Cause I think that I will go fishing," James replied.

I was so disappointed. When my parents found out that James was not going with us, they shared my disappointment.

By July, James and I were planning our first vacation. We decided to go the Smokey Mountains in Tennessee. We shared a wonderful week there, and I felt that we were on track to have a strong marriage.

SEPTEMBER 1969

One of my dreams came true. James and I bought our first house. It was a good neighborhood, and one of my neighbors became a very good friend. Before I passed the test for my driver's license, she drove me wherever I needed to go. She helped me to get a job where she was employed. She was working at a nursing home. So we went travelled about 25 miles each way.

I had the help from my neighbor to pass my test for my driver's license. The only vehicle James and I owned was his 1969 Chevy truck, which was a stick shift. I had only driven a stick shift or straight drive on my Grandpa's farm in one of his junked vehicles and was never moved. James tried to teach me how to drive with a clutch, but I just did not feel comfortable with it. My neighbor allowed me to use her car. I was so proud that I had only missed one question on my test. Finally I had my driver's license.

After a few conversations with James, he agreed to buy a car with an automatic transmission for me to drive. We bought a used 1965 Ford Fairlane in turquoise blue. My own car, and I loved it! I drove that car until it simply quit. But for a couple of years, and with my neighbor quitting her job, I had my own transportation.

EARLY 1971

I decided to quit my job, stay home, and work in my house. I really enjoyed being home for a few months. Over the next few months, I began experiencing an uncomfortable feeling in my stomach. I had never felt this before. *Can I be pregnant? Am I going to have a baby?*

"James, I think that I may be pregnant, "I said.

"Why?" he asked with disbelief.

"I have not had a regular monthly period for some time, and I think that I should go to the doctor. My clothes are getting tight, and I am gaining weight," I said.

"But you have done this before," James said.

"I understand that, but I have an appointment at the doctor's Friday morning," I said, "and I want you to go with me."

"Okay," James said with no argument.

***

After the tests at the doctor's office, James and I sat in the waiting room for the results. I was so hopeful and anxious.

The nurse called me back to the examining room. "Tawana, you're pregnant."

I began to cry. I practically ran to the waiting room to tell James. I was going to be a mom, and James was going to be a dad. The man of my dreams, the one I loved with all my heart and soul, and the man of my life, was the father of my baby.

That weekend, James and I went shopping for maternity clothes. Everyone was excited. There was going to be a baby in the family.

My next appointment was scheduled in three months. I experienced pregnancy symptoms and all that went with it. After a month, I decided to go back to see the doctor, just to see how I was doing.

After the examination, the doctor brought James and me to his office.

"Tawana," my doctor stated, "I would like to speak to you and James. I have some bad news."

"What is it?" I asked. I started to cry.

"You are not going to have a baby," the doctor said.

"YES! I am going to have a baby! What do you mean that I am not pregnant? You told me that I was pregnant!" I screamed.

"The test was misread," the doctor calmly stated.

"What do you mean misread?" I asked.

"Unfortunately, it is one of those things that happens sometimes," the doctor said.

"You made a mistake?" I asked not completely understanding.

"Tawana, you want a child very badly, don't you? When a woman wants a child very badly, it can overwhelm her body, and her subconscious allows her body to take on the symptoms of a pregnancy," the doctor explained.

I have never heard anything like this. *Is this another battle for me?*

James tried to be encouraging and kept telling me not to worry about it. James never realized how much I wanted this baby. *I wanted a baby so much that I tricked my body into believing that I was pregnant? How could this be?*

The disappointment was overwhelming for me. I had to sell my maternity clothes and put my faith in God for my future. I held onto the belief that time does have a way of healing and helping a person get over the hurt that comes to you in life. This was another low point for me, and I put my faith in God and prayed that his way would heal my broken heart. I knew then and know now that God can totally save you and give you peace.

CHAPTER 6

SUMMER 1970

James and I were getting along fairly well. He was doing what he wanted to do and when he wanted to do it. I accepted it, and was just staying at home.

I still had trouble with my weight and figured that I would always have a battle with it. I still was not pregnant, and I wanted a baby so badly that I cried myself to sleep at night. All I wanted was to be a housewife and mother. *What if it doesn't happen to me? Maybe I don't deserve to have these things in my life.*

Another nursing facility was being built and was due to open in the late fall. I decide to apply for a position and was hired. I was thrilled. I would be working on the 3 to 11 shift. It seemed to be perfect, since that was the same shift that James worked. It meant that we would get home at about the same time.

Things worked well. I liked being back in the workforce, and it got me out of the house. But more importantly, I found it to be very rewarding. I loved it! All the employees became one big family. A few months passed, and I had the opportunity to work day shift. It was a change, but I accepted it.

Working on day shift, I met a young woman that became my best friend. Through our work, we bonded quickly with each other. It was a rare thing to happen, but we became friends almost instantly. We became almost inseparable. We worked together, and then we would be on phone for hours.

We were even teased about it, but we just laughed. Little did I know that later in my future God had a hand in bringing about our friendship.

***

YEARS LATER

It was the first of November, and I was 25 years old. My friend, Dee, her husband, James, and I began to spend time together. She and I always had things to talk about, and James and Dee's husband liked to go fishing. With the holidays approaching, she and I went Christmas shopping, wrapped packages, and made bows. We made candy and cookies together— then and through the years to come. We shared so many things as best friends. As the years went by our friendship became very strong. I trusted her, and we shared our innermost thoughts and feelings with each other and never worried about them being shared with someone else.

As our lives changed, the baby that I always wanted seemed to be a dream. My siblings were growing up and going out on their own. One of my sisters had been married a few years and had been blessed with a beautiful little girl. She was my parents' first grandchild, and she was loved and spoiled.

I prayed that I would have my own baby, but instead it was God's plan that I became a godparent. I also became a loving aunt to my namesake and others when my other siblings got married and their families grew. I was happy for all of them but still felt a twinge of jealousy. I wanted a baby so badly.

For years I kept going to the doctors and hoping to conceive. James and I tried everything. I took fertility drugs and took my temperature to see if I was ovulating. I knew everyone's thoughts. *What's the matter with Tawana? What's the matter with Tawana's baby basket? Something must be wrong with Tawana.* Sometimes the thoughts were vocalized. The words hurt so badly that I found myself putting up walls to protect myself. I internalized the hurt and kept it inside.

I finally decided to refocus and to accept my life without a child. James was my life and my home. I told myself that my marriage was based on each other, not children. So I decided to go back to work and to having my own money again. I wanted to have my own money to buy my own clothes and things for my house.

Even with a job and my own money, I felt incomplete. I blamed myself for not being able to give James a baby. He was so good with all the nieces and nephews, and it just depressed me more. In addition to seeing myself as inadequate, I disliked my body. I had gained weight. I felt less than a complete woman.

I really believe that the only internal peace a person can have is through God. But at this time of my life, I wasn't ready to do that just yet. I felt I had a lot of other things to do with my life.

CHAPTER 7

LATE FALL 1984

Losing weight was important to me. I decided that I had to take control of the situation, and along with some girls at work, I went on a mission to lose weight. I was a little skeptical but after a few months, Dee and I had lost noticeable weight.

James and I planned to go to Florida for the Christmas holiday. I had lost so much weight that I was able to shop for cute clothes—in size medium instead of large! I loved it. So, with my new look and new clothes, I was ready for our trip. I was pleased that no one could believe their eyes when they saw me. I loved the way I looked.

James did not have much to say about my weight loss. I didn't really care because I just felt so good about myself. My friend Dee was happy with her weight loss too, and we hoped to never gain back the weight.

SPRING–SUMMER 1985

One day when James and I were looking through the local newspaper, we saw a house that we sort of liked. Then I accidently found some paperwork that James had placed in a drawer. To my surprise, he had placed a down payment on the house. He had not even discussed this with me. After sixteen years of marriage, he did not think that he should consult me. I was furious.

When James came home, I was so angry. James calmly told me that we could go look at it, and if I decided that I did not like it, he wouldn't buy it.

The next morning, James and I went to look at the house. Immediately on pulling into the driveway, I loved it. It was all I had ever wanted. It was a brick house that had a big kitchen with built in cabinets, three bedrooms, and a garage. I agreed that we should buy it. I was so excited.

We were moving again, but to my dream house. I worked hard to add finishing touches to the house and was able to buy things to really make the house perfect.

Dee helped me unpack, and I was so happy. Through all the work, I started having some untimed bleeding. It wasn't too heavy, but it was enough to bother me. I tried to pass it off as being due to all the work I had been doing and the excitement of everything. I would work at the nursing facility all day and then rush home to work on my new home.

One June morning, I was getting ready for work my shift, which was 6 am to 2 pm. I really liked this shift, even if it meant waking up at 4 am. My morning was as usual, when I started to walk down the hallway, and I became so weak I could hardly walk. It scared me. What was wrong? It must be fatigue. What about the on and off bleeding?

I immediately called the 24/7 service for my gynecologist. I explain my situation. The doctor called me back quickly, and he suggested that I be at his office as soon as it opened.

I called in sick to work, and before I woke James, I lay down on the couch and fell asleep. I had a dream. I dreamed that I was pregnant and gave birth to a beautiful baby girl with lots of dark brown hair. She was so perfect.

When I awoke, all I could think about was that dream. I woke James, and he and I arrived at the doctor's office early. The doctor did an examination and ran some tests.

James and I waited for the doctor to come in and talk to us.

Very shortly the doctor came into the room, and said, "Tawana, you're pregnant."

I laughed and said, "There ain't no way. I've been bleeding for a month. You can't do that and be pregnant."

"You are pregnant," he said, "but you're miscarrying."

I was shocked.

"We need to do a DNC. We'll schedule you for the procedure in the morning."

I was numb. I was one big mess. I cried all the way home. James went on to work, and I was there alone. As soon as Dee got home from work I called her. Like the best friend that she was, she took off from work the next day to be with James and me at the hospital.

I packed a few things and prepared myself for the outpatient procedure. As soon as I arrived at the hospital, more blood tests were done. The test results were the same. I was pregnant. The DNC had to be performed. I was simply bleeding too much. I was so afraid, but James and Dee were there to comfort me.

The surgery was to be just a few hours , but James waited as long as he could, and he had to go on to work. Dee told him not to worry—she was staying.

When the procedure was completed, the doctor went to the waiting room to discuss things with James.

"Where is Tawana's husband?" the doctor asked Dee.

"He just left to go to work. He had to leave. Is everything okay?" asked Dee.

"You need to call James to come back. We preformed the DNC, but we couldn't find the fetus. The blood tests still indicate a pregnancy. We suspect that the fetus is attached to the outside of her fallopian tube. This explains why there was little pain. While she is under the anesthetic, we need to perform a complete hysterectomy," the doctor explained and returned to do my surgery.

When I came out of recovery, I knew something more had happened.

"Tawana, given the circumstances, a complete hysterectomy was the only option," the doctor explained.

I couldn't believe what was being said to me. *How could this be? I have been married for eighteen years now, and now that I'm thirty-five years old, this was my only chance to have a baby!*

The five days I stayed in the hospital were spent thinking about my dream and the beautiful baby girl in it. I felt that she was real, and I knew that my beautiful baby daughter was in heaven. I tried not to be angry, but all I ever wanted was to have children. But I believed that God gave me a glance of her, and I decided that He must have needed her more. My faith was challenged, but I knew in my heart that God always knows best. And what if I had carried her full-term and then had to give her up ?

As devastating as this was to me, my faith and trust in God's decision told me that this was not the end of my life. By my faith, I accepted God's decision, and in a few weeks, I went back to work and tried to put the experience behind me.

THREE YEARS LATER—SUMMER 1988

Time had passed quickly, and I guess I had tried to settle into my life as it was. But I was restless. I became restless with my job, which I really loved, but I felt that I wanted something different. One Saturday afternoon, James and I were riding in our car and just enjoying the pretty weather when we drove by a cosmetology school.

"James! Stop! I want to go in and get some information about their classes," I said.

"Why?" James asked.

"Just stop. I'm going in to check it out," I answered.

Driving back home, James and I discussed the information, but by the time we arrived home, the subject was dropped. A month went by, and it was all I thought about. I decided to quit my job and get my license as a hairdresser. I gave my two-weeks' notice and signed up for the classes starting in August.

Dee was surprised. I was surprised at myself! But this was something that I had always wanted to do. That, or be a nurse. I decided to go for it. I was nervous about going back to school since I had been out of school for twenty years, but I was sure that I could do it.

The training took about eleven months. During classes, I meet wonderful people, and many of the patrons became my friends. I enjoyed learning, and even though I had the jitters when I gave my first haircut, my instructor was great, and I knew that I was going to be a hairdresser.

The months flew by, the holidays came and went, and a new year had begun. I felt good about the coming year. I would finish my classes and take my state cosmetology exam in May.

Time moved quickly, and before I knew it, it was May. I was so nervous about the test. Dee agreed to be my hands-on model for testing, and she was there to offer support to me as well. The tests went well, but I was still worried. But after six weeks of waiting to hear if I had passed the test, I received the results in the mail. I couldn't open the letter. James did.

"You passed!"

CHAPTER 8

AUGUST 1989

In August, I started working at a beauty salon. I could not believe that I was already there. I offered facials, manicures and of course anything to do with hair. I really enjoyed my job and slowly things began to pick up for me. I started to build a clientele.

With school starting, my nieces wanted Aunt Tawana to do their hair. I told my sister Sue to bring them to the shop on Saturday morning. She arrived with both girls. I had finished one's hair and was processing the other's when I received a phone call.

"Tell Sue to get home fast!" yelled Sue's sister-in-law in the phone.

"What? What is wrong?" I asked but was interrupted.

"Sue's house is on fire! Tell her to get home as fast as possible!" she yelled.

I looked at Sue and said, "Your house is on fire! You've got to get home! Now! Leave the girls here and go!"

"I'll call you," Sue said as she hurried out the door.

The girls wanted to know when they were going to be able to go home. I tried to explain to them that when I finished their hair, I would take them home. This seemed to satisfy them for the time being.

Hours passed. Finally I got a phone call from Sue.

"Don't bring the girls back until I call you," Sue said.

"Is it bad?" I asked.

"It's a disaster. Everything has been destroyed," Sue said through tears. "You should tell the girls that it is bad."

"I will," I said as she hung up the phone.

The girls were confused.

"Girls, do you understand that your house was on fire?" I asked.

They both nodded yes. "Well, it's bad. Your house was burnt really badly. So when you see it for the first time, it's okay to scream, run, holler, and cry or whatever you may feel like doing," I explained. "Do you understand?"

The girls nodded yes.

Finally, Sue called and told me to bring the girls home. I don't think that any of us were prepared for what we saw. It was complete devastation. We all cried. Sue was in shock. We walked around and looking at the destruction of the fire. Things were fused together on the wall, and items were melted into unrecognizable shapes.

Fortunately, they had a little camper that was unharmed. We were thankful no one was hurt, and we thanked God that no one lost their life. The girls did lose their little hamster, but we knew that God would continue to guide us through this, and the challenges to come. It was going to be a chore to go through clothes, wash them, and salvage anything that could be saved. The girls weren't able to start on the first day of school, but the community pulled together with donations of food, clothing, and money.

It had been a week since the fire. It was Sunday afternoon, and James and I had just arrived home from helping Sue and her family. Even though James had been sick, he was trying to help. As we walked inside our house, the phone rang, and I answered it.

When I answered the phone, and I hear a young girl's voice speaking.

"Hello. I am calling to ask about the Campbell family," she said. "I am doing a family tree, and I was hoping to get information. Can you help me?"

"You probably need to speak with my husband, James. Hold on," I said.

I handed the phone to James. James talked to her for a few minutes. I could hear the small talk, but basically he told her that he wasn't sure that he could help her but that she was welcome to call back. James and I didn't discuss the phone call.

AUGUST 28, 1989—MY LIFE CHANGES

James and I were having dinner when the phone rang. When I answered, I recognized the same young voice from the weekend phone call.

"Hi. I'm calling back to talk to your husband," she said.

"Well, wait just a minute," I said.

I handed the phone to James.

"This is James," he said.

He was silent for a couple of minutes and then said, "No, she doesn't know. I never told her. She had no idea about anything."

James was quiet again and then said, "Yes. You can call me back later."

James hung up the phone and turned to me.

Without warning, I said sharply, "Was that your damn girlfriend?"

"No," James said calmly. "That was my daughter, and she has a twin brother."

I froze in silence. My heart was shattered instantly into what seemed like thousands of pieces, and one of the shattered pieces went straight under my right armpit. I was in shock!

Will I ever be the same as I once was? I don't even know me. I have been put in a box and put on a shelf for so long. I have had so many things to deal with, and now I have to deal with this! Will I ever have a sound mind? Only God knows! What will happen to me and James and now his kids?

Staring at James, I could not speak. He was trying to explain.

"It just happened. Long ago. They're 19 years old," James said.

"You are lying to me!" I screamed.

"No, I'm not," James replied. He turned and tried to call her back. He got a wrong number.

"Come on. We have somewhere we need to go," James said.

Going somewhere? Now? After what I have just heard? I was so numb with shock, I think that I just moved on his command.

We got in the car, and James drove to another small town. He pulled the car into a driveway, got out, walked up to the front door, and knocked.

"Oh, you must be the kids' father," I heard someone say.

"I need the phone number to get in touch with my daughter," I overheard James say.

James returned to the car with a phone number. We started back home. I was full of questions.

"Who were those people?" I asked.

"They're friends of the family," James answered.

Immediately after we arrived home, James called all his family and then his daughter. I was dying inside and just crying. I needed to talk to someone. I wanted to call Dee and my family. I knew that I could not call Sue, with her having just lost everything in the house fire. She had enough on her mind. So, I called Dee and asked her to come to see me.

When Dee arrived, I told her my nightmare. She was shocked and became angry. Dee offered to stay the night with me for support, but I insisted that she go home.

I couldn't sleep and life became wheels of motions. I slept in the guest bedroom and didn't shower or comb my hair for days. Every day, Dee checked on me and finally made me get out of bed, shower, and get myself together. But after she went home, I was still in the middle of my upside-down world.

I found myself reliving every moment of my marriage. Second guessing comments and excuses. I remembered when James and I were cleaning his truck and I found a picture of two little kids.

"James, whose picture is this? And who are these kids?" I asked.

"Oh, it's someone I work with. He was showing me a picture of his kids. He must have left it. Just put it back. I'll give it to him Monday," he responded quickly.

I had held his children's picture in my hand and did not know.

James kept telling me it happened a long time ago. He made it sound so simple and like I should just get over it. My husband had an affair nineteen years ago that resulted in two children, and I should just get over it? All I wanted was to have my own family. I prayed and asked God to give me children, even if it meant a baby left on my doorstep. I did not expect to get them when they were nineteen years old and grown!

"How long have you known about the children, James?" I asked.

"One day I went to the post office, and I had received a letter with a picture of them. Their grandmother started sending pictures of them when they were about three years old," James said. "She did that for a while, and then suddenly the letters stopped."

"James, how could you keep this a secret? Our whole life together has been a lie," I cried. "Nothing for twenty-two years has any value. It has been all deception and lies!"

James just looked at me. I don't think he knew what to say.

"I am a real sympathetic person, and I would have wanted to be involved with their lives. All I ever wanted was a family!" I choked out through tears.

How am I ever going to get over this, through this, or accept this?

As time passed, James, his daughter, and his son began to talk often. I had to share James with them. He had his family. The kids were living in California, where they had grown up. The daughter was married and had two babies, and the son was single but lived with his sister and her family. But I overheard James's phone conversations with his daughter, and it was clear that she wanted to visit or possibly move near him.

It seemed all of us had our own battle. My sister Sue had lost everything in the house fire. While visiting me, my sister Carol told me that her marriage was not going well. And now this for me.

This situation between James and me escalated the past accusations and abuse to a new level. When James had decided that I wasn't worth hitting anymore, he became verbally abusive. The bruises healed, but the verbal abuse never went away. I believe that time does have a way of healing all wounds, but it only forms scars to cover the pain.

CHAPTER 9

M om came to visit me. I had always been close to my mom, and it was great to have her near. And somehow people started coming to our home and hanging out. Maybe it was family connection, but it felt like everyone was supposed to be there. I guess my family felt that if they were there, it was going to help ease the pain for all.

One night when James and I had guests, I went back to our bedroom. I felt an unnatural coldness. In the room we had a ceiling fan, and I looked up to see if for some reason it was on. When I looked, there sitting on one of the blades was something that looked like a fairy. I looked away and looked again. It was still there. It was laughing and talking to me.

"You are not going to make it," it laughed.

What in the world? Am I losing it? Is this the Devil to push me on over the edge?

For what seemed like days, that fairy was in the room sitting on the ceiling fan blade, laughing at me, and telling me that I was not going to make it!

I felt that I was between good and evil. I prayed every night for God to help me to cope. James just did not understand why I was so upset, angry, and confused. I felt so deeply in my heart and soul. I felt cheated in every way. I had to believe that God would fix this mess some way. I was searching for instant relief, but it wasn't going to be a quick fix. I wasn't able to work, and, fortunately, they told me to take all the time I needed.

I was sure that I was slipping from reality. Maybe I felt that my reality was too much to face. I was in trouble because I didn't know how I was going to handle this or anything more. All I knew was that I had to stay in prayer and let God take care of me. I did not lose my faith. One night, I was led to this scripture:

"God is our refuge and strength, a very present help in trouble..." Psalms 4:1 KJV

That night, with scripture in my mind and my heart, the fairy was gone. I never saw it or heard its words in my mind again. I gave thanks to God and his power of healing.

***

A few days had gone by, and James told me that we needed to go for a ride. Mom was there with me.

I was standing in the kitchen when suddenly I felt like I was having a heart attack. The pain was so sharp, and it went through my chest. It was so painful that my knees buckled, and I hit the floor. Mom helped me sit on a chair, and she was very concerned. She knew that something was wrong.

"Mom, I am fine. I just need to put my shoes on, and we'll go," I said.

"Tawana, this is not normal," Mom said.

Mom and I got in the car with James, still uncertain about where we were headed.

"James, where are we going?" I asked.

James never answered. He just drove.

Finally, James pulled in front of an old, big building. Mom and I exchanged puzzled looks.

"What is this, James? And why are we here?" I asked. I thought that this must be where James came with his buddies to camp out or hunt. He didn't have any trouble finding the place. He had been here before.

"You don't have to get out here because you already know what this place is!" James snapped.

"What do you mean, James?" I asked. "I don't know where we are and why we're here."

Without warning, James turned and looked at me with a coldness in his eyes and said,

"Sure! You know exactly what this is! This is one of the places you come to with your boyfriends!"

I was speechless.

He looked at Mom and said, "Do you know what kind of daughter you have? Your daughter is a whore!"

Mom's mouth dropped open with shock. I was totally speechless. I had seen this side of James behind closed doors, but for the first time, he was airing his true side in front of my mother. I was devastated and embarrassed. It was one thing for James to attack me privately, but now he was attacking me in front of my mother! Outside the doors of our home, I always made James look good, and I put on a front that everything was okay. We appeared to be the perfect couple to all who knew us. Dee was the only person who knew how bad our situation really was.

"James! You get us back to the house right now! You are crazy!" Mom yelled.

James started laughing.

"Now, James! I mean it! You turn this car around and get us back to the house!" Mom yelled.

She and James started yelling at each other, and at the same time, James just laughed. All I could do was cry.

When we got back to the house, Mom and I jumped out of the car.

"You are going back to Florida with me!" Mom said. "Where did James go?"

"I guess he went on to work," I answered.

"You are going back with me, Tawana," Mom repeated. "I have a couple of more days. That will give you time to pack, and we'll leave together."

"OK. Yes. I'll go," I said.

When James came home for work, he saw the packed suitcases.

"What's going on here?" he asked.

"I think that it is the best thing for me, James. I am going to leave for a while," I answered, trying to remain calm.

James answered with one of his favorite threats to me, "If you leave, I will put your shoes away! Understand?"

I knew exactly what he meant. He had said that to me so many times, each time with more conviction. He meant that he would kill me.

I had lived in fear for so long. Each time that James and I talked, I thought that we were moving forward. But each episode was a setback, and our situation was not really improving. I knew that running from the situation would not fix it, just prolong it.

I felt trapped. I lived in constant fear of doing something wrong, of saying the wrong word. Just looking a certain way would set him off in one of his tirades. The accusations grew more intense and more often. The abuse was now at a different level. It didn't matter who I was with or what I was doing—if James had something to say, he exploded on me at that moment. I found myself more and more afraid of what he might do.

I knew the daily walk of 'walking on eggshells.' It's not an easy walk. You face each day with an internal fear hidden with a smile. At any moment the abuse can begin. *What will he accuse me of doing this time? Will he hit me? What if I cannot defend myself? What if someone finds out?* Your defenses are broken. *What if I do leave? Where do I go? What will I do? Can I make it on my own? What if...*

After a couple of days, Mom decided not to go back home and instead to stay for a while longer. I was glad for that. Maybe she saw how quickly James could change and appear that he was regretful. I knew that I had two choices. Leave him or forgive him. If I forgave him, I needed to stay with him. After twenty-years, when it was good, it was good, but when it was bad, it was horrible.

I was relieved when James went to work, because it gave me a chance to be alone and try to figure out things. Everything was closing in on me: James's abuse, his affair, and now his children from this affair. I felt overwhelmed. Also, I knew that his children wanted to come to visit us. *How was I to handle his two children visiting with the two babies? Do they want to come and take over my home? How will James treat me if they visited?*

My thoughts were spinning, and the situations were blurring into one nightmare. I decided that I should go see a counselor. Mom agreed that it was a good idea, and she went with me.

The next morning, Mom and I drove to a counselor's office. We stood in the office, and I looked at the receptionist.

"I would like to talk with a counselor," I said.

"You need to have an appointment," she said with an attitude.

"So, you mean that I if were standing here with a gun to my head, I would need an appointment?" I asked and broke into a flood of tears.

"Just a minute," she said. She stepped into another office. Out came a man with her.

"Can I help you?" he asked.

"I need to talk to someone," I said through my tears.

He escorted to me to his office. He listened as I completely unloaded my situations to him. I explained to him what a terrible time I was experiencing. He listened. He was so kind and offered a prayer for me to have strength for me to get through this. I must have been in his office over an hour, but I never received a bill for his consultation. I still thank God for that man who showed compassion and took that time to listen to me. On that day, that man cared and was a lifeline for me.

God is my refuge and strength...

Mom and I went home. We were having a light lunch, sitting, and talking about things when she and I became quiet. We both felt it. There was a calmness that entered the room. We looked at each other.

"Do you feel it?" I asked.

"Oh, yes! What do you think it could be?" Mom asked.

I froze for a moment. I knew. It was the presence of God in my house.

"What is happening to you?" Mom asked with surprise.

"Mom, I am so calm. God is healing me," I answered.

For the next few minutes, I felt God's healing hands working inside of me. *I felt a miracle!* God worked from the top of my head through my body. When He got to my chest area and my heart, I felt Him putting my shattered pieces back together. Remember how I had felt that piercing pain under my armpit? God went there and got that piece to bring it back and make me whole. Only God could make my heart whole again, and He did. I felt my heart become soft and pliable, and my heart was filled with love. The anger that had taken over my life was being removed and replaced with love. It continued down my body and to my feet. Mom was praising and worshipping God. She felt the miracle of God and saw it happen before her eyes.

That moment was a pivotal point in my life. I did not know the magnitude of the miracle. I had been given a book by Marie Shrophire, *God Cares*

About Your Tears. One passage that I embraced was "Don't ask why this has happened to me, but ask what God wants you to learn from this. My faith tells me that He will show you if you really want to know."

It was a miracle! God's healing had taken place in me. I will always be thankful. I thanked God for filling me with His love and kindness. And at that time in my life, I didn't have any idea of God's future plan for me or what was ahead. But I did know that I would listen.

I believe.

"To him the porter openeth; and the sheep hear his voice: and he calleth his own sheep by name, and leadeth them out." John 10:3 KJV

CHAPTER 10

Even though James had not admitted it, I knew through rumors and telltale signs that James's children were coming for a visit. *How will I get through this?* The voice inside told me, "I will guide and direct you." I knew that it would be difficult, but I had God on my side.

So in the next few weeks, I started to talk about the kids' visit, and James and I communicated more. We talked about them and actually became excited about their visit. I actually felt excited, too. I had always prayed that if God left a baby at my door, I would raise it as my own. Maybe this was his plan. I had no idea of the bigger plan he had for me.

It was confirmed. By the middle of October, I needed to get the house in order. James and I were having guests. We needed another bed set and a baby bed for a three-year-old and a nine-month-old.

I wanted everything to look festive with fall colors. Decorating included pumpkins and mums, and I worked hard to prepare rooms for our guests. Mom checked on me to see how I was doing with things and recognized that I was overwhelmed with excitement. I had wanted to pick out two cards and two roses to lay on their beds for when they walked into their rooms. Maybe it was a bit extreme, but I was never known for doing things halfway. When they arrived, everything looked so inviting, and I know that they felt it, too.

I began to think about being an instant mom and grandmother. *How will I get used to the sound of being called Mom or Mama?*

I was still processing that I was going to have two grown kids (nineteen years old) and two babies in my house for two weeks. I was nervous about it, but I kept repeating to myself '*I can do all things through Christ who strengthens me.*' *Philippians 4:13 KJV*

It seemed normal now to have telephone conversations with them. In our last conversation, I told them that I needed pictures so I that could recognize them at the airport when they arrived. James and I planned to meet them at the airport. They called the night before to make sure we would be there to pick them up.

***

We left the house at 9:30 am to head to the airport. The airport was about an hour and half away from us. I don't think that I had ever felt such a somber feeling in my house as I had that morning, and I knew the ride to the airport would feel the same.

The silence in the car was broken when James said, "I don't want you to make a scene about anything."

I couldn't believe I had heard those words. *After all I've done and been through with this, he has the nerve to tell me that?*

"James, you are not going to talk to me that way today," I said.

He glanced over at me, and I continued. "And you are going to ride in the back seat with your daughter, and I am driving back home."

James did not have anything more to say.

We finally arrived at the airport and made our way to the gate. The sign showed that the flight was on time. The plane would be landing in about 30 minutes. My life as I knew it was going to change in about 30 minutes. It was countdown. Nothing would be same as when I left my house this morning. I suddenly felt faint and had to sit down. I thought *Let James take charge.* I could see signs of nervousness in James, and I was so nervous that I wasn't sure that I could get through this.

Waiting for them to get off the plane was nerve-wracking for me. All the 'what if's raced through my mind. I realized that James was probably thinking about a lot of 'what if's too. I was sure the children had questions and wanted answers. *I* wanted answers. I wanted an apology. Here we were standing at the airport to meet his children from his affair, and James still had not even apologized to me. Not one hint of "I'm sorry for putting you through all this." I believed that he was only sorry that his long-time secret was now known.

***

Passengers were exiting the plane. *Where were they? What was taking so long? Did they miss the plane?* Then I saw James's son. I knew it was him. He was an exact image of James. The daughter (twin sister) did look like her brother, but she looked even more like James's paternal grandmother. I recognized them both immediately. Here walking toward us were two kids carrying two little babies. They ran to James and hugged him. They turned to me, and with smiles and tears, we hugged each other. We all were crying, even the babies. It was so emotional. *What was ahead for all of us?*

It seemed to take forever to get back home. On our way there, we talked small talk, chatting about the flight and the weather, with a few other words here and there. The son and I connected on the ride home. When we arrived, they were so excited. I was so proud of their rooms, and they were very pleased with the way everything looked. They couldn't believe the cards and all the other little things that I had done for their visit. They were so grateful.

They told me that was the nicest thing anyone had ever done for them. Later I would find this to be true.

I watched James's children and the two babies as we put the little ones to bed. *Will they call me Mom or Mama? When?* I had asked God so many times to have someone leave a baby on my step, and I would raise as my own. It seemed that He had not only done that, but He had brought two babies—and two grandbabies at the same time!

We got settled in for the night, and the babies were in bed. The four of us gathered in the living room and started talking. Conversation turned into asking questions. One of the biggest questions from the kids was why their dad did not try to get custody of them. That was a big question for me too. I would have loved to have raised them. Of course, James had a vague answer that really didn't satisfy any of us. But it was late at night, and we all were tired.

For the first time in months, James and I went to bed together. We had not been sleeping together, and sleep was all we shared that night. I asked him to stay on his side of the bed.

The next morning, I heard the kids in the kitchen fixing something to eat. I realized that I had to share my house and my world with them. I wasn't sure I was happy to be doing that, but I thought, *Tawana, you can handle this for a couple of weeks.*

James took his two-week vacation during their visit. There were lots of people to see and places to go. The plan was to introduce them to new families. They must have felt overwhelmed, but they were excited.

By the end of the first week, we were comfortable with each other. We had stayed busy with visiting and other activities. We were headed to the amusement park when James's son called me Mom. The word struck me. I looked at him, and he looked at me. Nothing was said. I thought that it was just a slip of the tongue. We continued to talk, and he again addressed me as Mom. I did like the idea of being that close to him and his sister. They must have discussed it and agreed to call me Mom. James thought that it was great. But I was overwhelmed by it, because it seemed like it was being repeated by everyone. It was too much for me.

"I don't want to hear the word Mom one more time!" I screamed.

The kids were shocked. "What's wrong?"

"I just think that it has been too much too soon," James explained. "Maybe someday, but not right now."

The kids seemed confused, and later that evening, they indicated that they wanted to talk to me.

"We've talked about this. We do not want to have any kind of 'step' words between us. You are our Mom and from this point on, you are Mom to us, and we are your son and daughter."

We all started to cry. I knew that I was instantly a Mom and Mama. God knew when all this would happen. Maybe anytime earlier, I would not have been able to adjust and accept them. All in God's timing. I was falling in love with these kids. Only God Himself could have put all the pieces of my shattered heart back together and fill it with the love and kindness I needed for the challenge ahead. God had been preparing me all along.

From that moment on, I knew that I was to be a Mom and Mama role-model for them. I needed to always be there with an open mind and heart to comfort them as they needed. As a mom to them, I needed to advise them when they asked. I wanted to do my best!

The two-week visit neared its end. The daughter had a husband to get back to, but the son seemed to want to stay around longer. He had met a pretty girl at the fall festival and was falling for her quickly. He had asked her parents if she could come over to his parents' house. They were surprised to learn that Tawana and James were his parents.

The two weeks went by quickly. But by the end, I was ready for a break from all the busyness.

On the last night together, we had a late dinner and recapped the last two weeks. So many things we had shared and enjoyed doing! The nine-month-old baby had even learned to crawl during the visit.

The next morning was greeted with mixed emotions from all of us. The son asked to come back at Christmas to visit, and both kids wanted to spend the holidays with us! James and I got them to the airport and on the plane. They were on the way back to their home in California. But my life had been changed forever.

James and I had little to say to each other on the drive back home. I had an empty feeling, and it was just James and me again. My thoughts jumped from his children to my sister Carol, whose marriage was in trouble. I couldn't help but wonder what was going to take place for all of us.

CHAPTER 11

THE HOLIDAYS

It was decided that everyone would come to our house for Christmas. I loved making things look festive. And although I usually put up my artificial Christmas tree on Thanksgiving night, I decided I wanted a real Christmas tree this year. This would mean putting up the tree a little later. So the first week of December, James and I went together to pick out the perfect real Christmas tree.

I had so much fun decorating the house. I prepared for fifteen or 20 people to visit. I felt the more, the merrier. But it did mean cooking a big ham and fixing all the trimmings. It also meant a long Christmas list and lots of gift to buy.

A couple of days before Christmas, the kids arrived. Carol and her son were already with James and me. Mom was on her way. I knew that it was going to be one of the best Christmases ever, and it was. Once everyone had gone back to their homes, we continued for weeks to talk about what a great holiday it was.

Starting the new year, I was in for another change.

"My son wants to move here and live with us," James said.

"No way. I do not think that he should move here. And I don't think that he should live with us," I said.

"Well, he and I have talked a lot about it, Tawana," James said. "I told him that he can come and live with us."

"But I said no," I reminded James. I was not ready for that.

That was the last conversation about it, and the next thing I knew, James's son was living with us.

James was still working nights, and there were young men coming to the house to be with his son. I didn't like this, and felt like I was losing my house to him. I wasn't having empty nest syndrome, I was having 'invaded nest syndrome!' I told James that he would have to go on day shift if this was the way it was going to be. To my surprise, he did.

It didn't take very long for James's son to reconnect with the girl he met on his first visit. It was serious. She was graduating in May, and they wanted to get married right after. The source of the urgency was that she was pregnant, and in October, a baby girl arrived. She was a princess baby!

***

1992

After the excitement of the baby's arrival, I was at home when a feeling—a premonition—came over me. I knew that I was going meet the mother of James's children, because something bad was going to happen to one of them. I hoped that I was wrong, but I just knew. The feeling was so strong.

I helped with the baby when I could, and I watched her grow over the next year. She became my princess baby. The surprise came when we found out that my little princess was going to have a little brother.

***

1993

Almost a year later, we had a grandson, and he looked just liked James.

I was beginning to think James and I were going to make it after all, marriage-wise. We had a new reason. It was about being there for his children, and his daughter wanted to come out and live near him, too.

I knew that sooner or later, his daughter would want to be near him. After all these years of not even knowing their dad, both of his kids wanted to be near him—but not before a tragedy happened.

It was in the middle of a mid-October night when I received the phone call no one wants.

"Your son has been in a car accident, and you need to come to the hospital as soon as you can," the nurse said. Both James and I were not prepared for this.

We arrived at the hospital, and the son's wife and his in-laws were already there. They were giving us the details on everything, when the doctor walked into the waiting room.

"The life support is keeping the oxygen going to his organs," he said, so matter-of-factly. "He's already brain-dead. There is no activity at all from his brain."

In shock, we all remain motionless. "Is he a registered as an organ donor? You'll have to make a decision on this," the doctor said.

The decision could only be made by his wife. It all seemed to happen in such a short amount of time. It was one of the hardest decisions she probably ever had to make. We all decided to support her, but she had to decide.

He was such a young, strong man. The question of what to do was written with worry on her face. The doctor gave her just a few hours to make the decision. We had a group prayer and prayed for guidance to make the right decision. A couple of hours went by that seemed forever.

"I've made my decision. He never voiced to me that he wanted to be a donor. And since he had never said anything to me about it, I don't want one person to put a scratch on him. I will not allow anyone to take anything from him," she said strongly.

We knew we had to reach his sister and mother. Arrangements had to be made to get them here.

James called his son's mother. But I had to talk to her. She asked, "Can I come?"

"I think that you should come," I answered. "But there is one thing that you have to remember. You are his mother, but I am his mom." I knew that if I were to meet their mother it would be bad, but not this bad.

"Yes, that's OK," she said. "I'll make flight arrangements."

Dee was there for me and was standing next to me when I talked to her. After I hung up the phone, Dee asked, "Why are you being so nice to her? You should not let this happen."

I looked at her and said, "If I were the one in her shoes, I would hope someone would do the same for me. This is the last time she will get to see her son."

The twin sister was trying to find someone to help with her children. She finally decided to leave them with her husband and to not bring them to the hospital. She and her mom were on an airplane and headed my way.

We finally had all the arrangements made for his mother and twin sister to get to the hospital and had just told his wife that they would arrive after midnight, when the doctor walked in the room.

"Since he is not going to be a donor," he said, "we need to disconnect life support. You all need to say your goodbyes."

"It will be a few hours before his mother and his twin sister get here," we all said. "Can we just wait a few hours longer?"

"No," the doctor replied.

"Please!" we all pleaded. The answer was the same. They would only leave him on the machines longer if he were a donor, and since he was not, they couldn't allow any more time.

It's no wonder that people have problems with things like this when final requests are not in writing. Things do become complicated when a person can no longer speak for himself or herself.

In the midst of saying our goodbyes, I felt a burden for his twin sister and his mother.

I leaned over to him and said, "Your sister wants you to know that she loves you very much, and she is on her way." I kissed his cheek. "This kiss is from her."

I took a deep breath and said, "You have brought love and blessings into my life. I am so proud of you and so proud that you let me know the feeling of being a mom." I kissed his cheek again.

As I started to walk away, God spoke to me. "Tell him that his mother loves him."

I froze for a second and could not move from the spot where I was standing. I was startled by the words, but I knew in my heart that I had to do this. *Why?* I didn't have an answer.

I leaned back down and whispered in his ear, "I want to let you know that your mother is on her way to come to you. I can tell you that she loves you." I kissed his other cheek. With tears running down my face, flooding my eyes, I became weak, and Dee had to lead me outside the room. God and Dee were there for me. His mother and sister did not make it to the hospital to say their goodbyes.

We left the hospital, drove home, showered, and got back on the road to the airport to pick up his mother and sister. This would be the first time to come in contact with the mother of 'my' kids. She was the other woman. I couldn't think about that. We shared the one son.

I knew that this situation was going to be bad. James and I discussed how they should be told about having to disconnect life support. We agreed that he would tell them once we got through baggage claim and were back to the car.

I don't think I had ever walked so fast after we got to the baggage claim, and out the door we went. When we got to the car, his mother asked, "How is he doing?"

James looked at her and shook his head no. He went on to tell them that he was gone.

Their screams were bone-chilling, and their sobbing and crying never stopped on the way to the house. I had my own sobbing and crying in my heart as well.

There were many things to do. Where was everyone going to stay? What about the daughter-in-law and the children? What about cemetery plots?

***

FUNERAL SERVICES

At the funeral home, it was time for the family to go in for the private time. I was not ready for the intense cries and sounds. Here was a young man who had touched so many lives in so many ways. We were now paying our last respects to him. It was amazing to see how many people had grown fond of him in such a short time. The little ones didn't understand. They kept trying to find their daddy.

As we gathered under the tent with our family and our closest friends, I felt Dee's hand on my shoulder, and I knew she was there for me and James. She never left us during the whole service.

I could feel his mother's pain. I could hear his mother say over and over again, "I never got to tell him that I loved him!"

I looked at Dee, and she smiled. Dee and I walked to her side. I took her hand, pulled her aside, away from others, and said, "There is something that I need to tell you. Before they unhooked the life-support machine, I told him goodbye for you."

"What do you mean?" she asked.

"I told him that you loved him and you were on your way to him. I gave him a kiss on the cheek for you."

She started crying, and through tears she said, "Thank you! Oh, thank you! Thank you for doing that for me! Because of you, he knew that I loved him."

I cried and said, "He knew that."

She said, "You have been more of a mom in three years and showed him a love that was true," she cried. I reached out and gave her a hug.

I wept like a baby. I knew why God had me to do what I had done. He wanted me to bring closure to a hurting mother. I understood things better, and I thanked God for his direction.

The service was over. A young man's life had ended. All his loved ones were now trying to carry on without him. *What an impact he made in my life!*

CHAPTER 12

A couple of months went by. Our daughter-in-law had been out of town and was returning in a couple of weeks. I was excited for them to return. I had missed them.

Before she returned, I went over to her apartment to freshen things up and to make sure that her pantry was full.

I knew when she returned, she would face emptiness and loneliness after losing her husband. The oldest still wondered where Daddy was and constantly was looking for her dad. She kept asking, "Where's Daddy?"

"She needs to know that her daddy is in heaven," I told my daughter-in-law.

"Yes, I want her to know, and I'll tell her," she said.

"We should get some balloons and a toy and go to the cemetery and try to explain it her," I suggested.

"Since we do have a picture of her daddy on the stone, we could try to explain that he has gone to heaven," she said.

That's what we did. We told his daughter that we were sending him balloons, and we attached notes to the balloons, saying 'I love you, Daddy, and I miss you." We allowed her to take her time, and we decided to take as long as she wanted.

After about an hour, she looked at us and said, "I'm ready to send the balloons to Daddy now." She let them go, and we watched them as long as we could see them. We hugged, cried, and just sat there on the ground for a long time.

"I'm ready to go now," she said. She left the little bear at the base of the headstone, and as we walked away, she threw a kiss to him.

From that day forward, she never looked to find her daddy in a crowd because she knew he was in Heaven. I thank God for His wisdom that He gave me for her. Time has a way of moving on, and either you go with it or you'll be left behind in a sad moment of time.

Everyone deals with grief in their own way, and I was trying to be the mom and mama I thought I needed to be as I tried to cope with my own loss too. But once again, James started with his accusations. How was I going to go through this loss and endure James's endless accusations? If we went out to eat or to visit, James began with his usual comments:

"Who did you see today?"

"Who are you meeting?"

"Where are you meeting them now?"

It seemed that he'd say anything just to upset me. I tried to not get upset, but I was exhausted, and his accusations wore me down. I kept telling myself that I had not done any of the things that he accused me of, but he always manipulated the conversation to make me feel guilty.

The verbal abuse climbed to a new level. It became more frequent and more harsh. I found the verbal abuse to be more frightening to me than the physical abuse. The body forgets what it feels, but the mind never forgets what it hears. The physical abuse eventually fades away, but the verbal keeps replaying in your mind.

Today, as I write this book and remove the locks from the doors that I sealed so tightly, I can hear the words play back to me:

"You will never amount to anything."

"No one else would ever want you."

"You are worthless."

"If you ever try to leave me, I will put your shoes away."

These phrases played over and over until I believed them. Along the way, I believed James. I totally forgot who I was. Tawana had been put in a box and left on a shelf. Would I ever find me?

***

Time passed, and when our daughter-in-law met someone new, I was happy for her. He was a wonderful young man. He seemed to make her happy, and when he asked her to marry him, she said yes.

I helped with the planning for the big day. What a beautiful wedding! The children loved him, and everyone could feel the love and romance between them. James and I kept the kids for them while they were on their honeymoon. It was a good thing for me, but James continued with his crazy accusations.

"What did you do today?"

"Who were you with?"

"Why is dinner not ready?"

Having the children around did not stop James from accusing me of being unfaithful. How could I, even if I had wanted to?

James just refused to see that he had a good woman. Would he ever know that and really appreciate me? To everyone who knew us, we were that perfect couple—outside of our house. But behind closed doors, we were another couple. My closest friend, Dee, and my sister Carol knew things were not always the way they seemed.

I was a silent victim. Abuse is abuse. No one should go through it. Silent victims can be men as well as women, but abuse is not acceptable for anyone.

***

Over the next couple of years, I gained over 100 pounds. I felt like I was drowning in a bottomless whirlpool, and I could not find a lifeline to grab to pull out of it. *Is this going to go on for the rest of my life?* So many times I thought of leaving in the middle of the night, but I didn't have anywhere to go. Where could I go where James wouldn't find me?

On a Friday night, James and I went out to dinner. I decided to sit beside of him instead of across from him.

"Who are you rubber-necking to see?" James asked.

"What? What do you mean? I don't know what you mean," I said trying to be calm.

"You know what I mean!" James snapped. "Who do you see? Looking for someone?"

I was crushed. I could not win for losing. I was sitting next to him, trying to be a loving wife. But no matter what I did, it was always wrong. I could not go out with him. James had become comfortable in being abusive to me in front of family and now strangers. What was I going to do? *I don't want to just sit home all the time!*

When we arrived home, James and I had a horrible fight. James hit me.

"I told you a long time ago, you will never hit me again," I yelled at him. "Do you hear me? Don't you remember? You said I wasn't worth your fist anymore!"

James left and went to work. After he left, I packed enough clothes for a week. I walked out the door and left. I was so nervous! Why was I feeling guilty? I hadn't done anything wrong.

It was a vicious cycle. I loved James, and when he would say that it wouldn't happen again, I wanted to believe him. Many people have asked me that one question that is always asked: "Why didn't you just leave?" How does one answer that? It is part of the unworthy feeling you take on yourself. I was brought up in a time when you stayed during the tough times, and I believed that once you were married, nothing separated you except death. The words from my dad—"You made your bed, now you lie in it"—resonated with our generation's definition of marriage commitment.

Dee and I had a friend that we met, and she had told me that anytime I needed a place to stay, I could stay with her. She was so kind and allowed me to stay with her.

James went crazy when he arrived home, and I was gone. He did not know where I was. Dee stopped by to tell me that James was calling her to find out where I was staying. I could tell Dee was worried for her safety and our friend's safety. James was watching to see where she was going, thinking that she would lead him to me.

I knew that I could no longer stay there. I was putting her and Dee in danger. I realized that my only choice was to go back and try to work it out with James. I knew in my heart that I was supposed to forgive him and forget all this, but how could I do that? Maybe someday I could forgive—but I'd never forget.

I went back home.

"James, we need to talk like we have never talked before," I said.

"What is there to talk about?" James asked.

"What do you mean? We need to talk about everything," I said.

"Fine. We will talk over the weekend. Maybe we could go somewhere," James said.

"Okay. I think that is a good idea," I said in agreement.

On Friday, James took off from work. Suddenly, I felt afraid. I wondered what his motive was. Come Friday night, he took off work, and we headed out of town and got a hotel room. We talked about everything.

"James, I cannot continue to live every day in fear of you or what you might do. I never know what is going to set you off and we end up arguing," I said. "I know that, in your mind and heart, you know that all the things that you say and accuse me of are untrue."

"You are not Miss Perfect," he answered.

I thought, *Oh no! Remain calm.*

"No one is perfect, James," I said, "but I am not what you say I am, and you know it. Why do you feel the need to say those things?"

He had no answer.

Finally, he said, "I'll try harder not to do things or say things."

I wanted so much to believe him. I still had deep feelings for him. By now, my feelings were not as deep as they had been in the past, because those deep feelings had been blasted away with his infidelity and were lost in fear. I would never fully trust him again. I've always believed—and repeated to others—that you trust until someone gives you a reason not to trust anymore. That's when you are forced to make a choice in what to do.

"We have over twenty years of marriage. That is a long time to be with someone," I said. "Do you really want to work this out?"

"Yes," he answered.

I had been with James for a long time and felt as if my life has been built on one lie after another. My faith remained strong.

I held on to God's scripture, *There hath no temptation taken you but such as is common to man: but God is faithful, who will not suffer you to be tempted above that ye are able; but will with the temptation also make a way to escape, that ye may be able to bear it. 1 Corinthians 10:13 KJV*

I believe and profess that God will not let any more come on you than you can bear. He will make a way to escape.

***

James and I bought another house across the street. We were remodeling and working on it one morning, when I started to do some painting in the master bedroom. James was at the other end of the house working in the kitchen area. On the wall in the bedroom were black and white circles. I was having a hard time getting them covered. I put on a coat of paint, let it dry, and the circles were still there. I put another coat of paint and allowed it to dry. This time when the paint dried, I was sweeping the floor, and suddenly I felt a very strong wind blow through the room. I was sort of alarmed. I began meditating on God's word and praying and asking God to clean the house of any bad things or spirits that might be lingering there. I turned to block the door open and asked God to clear it out. I could hardly hold the bedroom door open. There was such a force. I could hear the rush of the wind going down the hallway and into the kitchen. The wood planks on the floor were rattling. The noise was so loud that I thought James was still in there. I looked, and there was no one. I knew that God had cleaned out the evil spirits in this house. I gave Him thanks.

This time when I went back to put another coat of paint on the wall, it covered the circles completely. What a fresh feeling! I cried with joy and peace.

We had been in the house for a couple of years, and not a lot had improved with us. James was still verbally abusive. I held onto my faith and God's words of wisdom, hope, and encouragement.

One morning, James started the day out by calling me names, and it continued to get worse. It was my day from hell. I wasn't sure what brought it on, but he was relentless. He started accusing me of being with someone the night before, and he knew that it was untrue. This went on for hours as he was getting ready to go to work.

It was just another day in my miserable life. James didn't eat anything; I followed him as he walked out to the car. He was screaming accusations the whole time. He got in the car and backed out of the driveway. I was never so glad to see him leave. I slid down on the bench on the porch and cried. Suddenly I felt the presence of a hand on my shoulder. It was Dee. It was as if she were there, but it was her presence that I was feeling. It was as if she had walked up behind me. When I felt her presence, I could only hear these words flowing from my mouth in a poem. I jumped up and got pen and paper and started to write it down for her.

THE HANDS OF A FRIEND

The hands of a friend
Oh, let me see;
Where do I begin?
They're soft and gentle when you've been hurt, the hands of a friend.
When you are going through a sad time and you're in despair,
To feel the hands on your shoulder, you know that your Friend is there.
When you have fallen and you think no one cares,
You look and see and you know who is there.
Those carrying hands,
They can pick you up and help you stand,
That's the hands ... of a friend.
Now that all the blue is gone and the morning sun brings on a new dawn,
We look back and understand the care and Love in the...
HANDS OF A FRIEND...
Thank you, Dee, love you...

CHAPTER 13

The holidays came quickly, and we got through them. On New Year's Eve, James and I spent the day at a car dealership trying to reach an agreement on the purchase of a new van. Finally, all came together. We had a new van, and this bigger vehicle would be perfect for taking all the grandkids on trips and outings. We decided to plan an outing as soon as school was on spring break. We were excited.

***

IN THE ARMS OF GOD–JANUARY 2000

With this new year, I prayed for God to let it be a better year and help me get through it. As I tried to take down all the holidays' decorations and pack them away for another year, I realized how fragile life really was and that it should be handled with care.

February rolled around pretty quickly. On Valentine's Day, I worked to prepare a nice dinner for James for when he arrived home from work. I had the dinner all prepared, but he didn't get home until 2 am. Normally he was home around 11 pm. Of course when he finally arrived at home, words escalated into a yelling match.

"You shouldn't plan anything for me!" James snapped.

"Obviously not!" I yelled. "You sure don't plan anything for me!" The conversation stopped. We both seemed to have had enough.

By April, things had not improved. James started to talk about selling the house and downsizing. He even mentioned retiring and moving to Florida in the winter and keeping a condo in Indiana for the summer. I thought, *This sounds nice.* Why not? He had just turned 56 on his birthday, and he seemed to indicate that we were going to make it finally. Things were going to be OK!

All I could do was pray and hope.

***

In May, Carol and her husband came up to hold a revival at a little church where we had all attended as kids. It was like family. However, our beliefs were a little different. I wanted to go so badly, especially since they were staying at our house.

I put myself on a fast and locked myself away in a closet in prayer. I asked God for answers, direction, and deliverance. I was taught that a woman shouldn't cut her hair or wear pants. It was very confusing for me. All I wanted was to serve God and be a Christian. I was in spiritual warfare for two days, but finally I received 'word' that I knew God had given me. I left one church and went to the other one, where they were attending. I asked the pastor what I needed to do to be a member there, and he told me very kindly, "Just show up."

I thought that this could be the turn-around that I had been praying and hoping for. Things were improving some, and James seemed to be calmer in his actions. James had started attending church on and off with me. I just wanted us to be together and to be happy. Once we put the house on the market, we started to look at different places that had less maintenance and upkeep.

By the middle of June, we had several people look at the house. We were looking to downsize from a big house to a condo. It was going to be a big change for me. James was giving almost everything to his daughter for a huge yard sale. I had packed things away that were important to me, and

I was glad that I had kept aside the things most important to me, because we soon sold the house and moved into a condo.

Without warning, I began to see the 'ugly giant' rise up again in James, and the verbal abuse started again. It was such an unpredictable cycle. I suddenly had no say in any transaction.

By our July vacation, we were still unpacking things and getting things together at the condo. I found out that Carol and her husband were going to the Philippines on a missionary trip in September. They asked me if I would like to go with them and be part of the team. Oh, wow! What an awesome opportunity! Would James even consider this? I decided that I would find out. I waited until the weekend to discuss it with him.

On Saturday, I decided to talk to James about the trip.

"I got a call from Carol. She and her husband are planning a missionary trip to the Philippines," I said, "and they are leaving in September."

James did not make a comment.

"There will be Carol, her husband, and six more people. James, Carol asked me if I would like to go with them. I would be there for twenty-one days."

"I'm not going to pay for anything," James said.

"I'll need to get a passport and get my vaccinations for traveling outside the country, but I want to go," I said.

"If you want to go, you'll have to do it on your own," James said. "I guess that if you really want to do this, it's OK."

"Oh yes! I want to do this. It's the chance of a lifetime!" I said with excitement. I was so happy!

I was so excited, but a real battle was coming my way!

The church was so supportive with fundraisers for things that I needed, with donations and gifts for me for the trip. I continued to prepare for the trip.

James was starting with his endless accusations. He found something wrong in everything that I did and was done for me. I just stayed in my Bible and studied His word. With each word of verbal abuse, I kept these scriptures opened and quoted them over and over:

"No weapon that is formed against me shall prosper." Isaiah 54:17 KJV

That was my strength to get through the day and whatever I was facing at the time.

"No more come upon you than you can bear; He will give you a means of escape." 1 Corinthians 10:13 KJV

"GOD is our refuge and strength a very present help in trouble." Psalms 46:1 KJV

I thank God for always being there for me when no one else was around. He stayed closer than a brother. That was the only thing that kept me from going insane.

The closer the trip came to being a reality, the more accusations. But support and gifts kept coming in, and I eventually had enough funds for my airline tickets, with more than a thousand dollars left over. I believe that God does supply, and when He is for you, no one can take that away from you. Amen.

By the first of August, all I could think about was the trip. I thought of all the things I would be able to do for the team, and going on this trip was the chance of a lifetime. I was leaning on God for everything. In one month, I would travel half way around the world. Little ole me! *All things are possible with God." Matthew 19:26 KJV*

***

Just a week before I was to leave on my trip, James began to act differently toward me. He opened doors for me, he wanted to hold my hand in public, and he began to show me all this attention. This was so out of character.

"I want us to go to the jewelry store," James said. "I want to get you a new wedding band."

"A wedding band?" I asked.

"I never liked that one," James said, "so I want to get you another one."

"I don't need one. I like the one I have. It's a great one," I said.

However, we went to the jewelry store, and James picked out a new wedding band for me. It was too big and heavy and had to be resized.

"This is a big gold band, and I really don't like it," I said.

"This is the one I want you to have," James said.

It did not matter what I wanted. James had measurements made and ordered it.

"I don't want that ring," I said as we left the store.

James became very angry. "Oh, someone else has bought you a ring? Well, you don't need to wear that ring on your finger!"

James grabbed my hand and took my wedding band off my finger. I began to cry.

"Oh yeah. Go ahead. Cry over someone else," James accused.

I just looked at him. I thought, *This cannot be happening again!*

"Who is it? Who are you having sex with? Anyone I know? The only way you got all this money for this trip was to sell yourself! You've been going out and having paid sex! You are a whore!" James yelled.

The ring was ready for pick up in a couple of days. On Friday, James and I were back at the jewelry store to purchase the ring. I hoped that the ring wasn't ready, but it was. James put the ring on my finger, and when he did, I felt like he tied a heavy lock on my hand. It was so heavy and like nothing I had ever felt. I could not tell the difference between the weight of the ring and the feeling of heaviness. Was this heavy feeling going to be on me on my trip?

James decided that we should stay overnight in a hotel near the airport the night before my flight. I was relieved that James wanted to do this. I was very concerned that with an hour and half drive, he might have caused me to miss my plane. But the night before was just more of the same torment in my mind. My mind was in turmoil. I thought, *Oh God, I'm in your hands and getting ready to go on this missionary trip for you. Please keep me safe.*

We were having breakfast, and James was still acting out of character.

He was holding my hand. "How long have you been holding her hand?" a stranger asked James at the restaurant.

"Not long enough," James answered.

I just smiled and nodded my head. I was afraid that James would take that question and cause a scene. I just wanted to get on that plane and leave. We finished eating, and we were on our way to the airport. I got checked in and had some time to wait. James was still holding my hand, but it was with anger. I could feel the pain coming from him. I thought, *What is he going to do when they start announcing boarding?*

The announcement was made. My flight was called. I stood up to walk to the gate, and my dread became reality. James started yelling at me.

"Do you have to go half way across the world to call me and tell me you are getting a divorce?" He yelled. "You are afraid of what I will do to you!"

I was so humiliated. People were staring at us. I just started walking because all I wanted to do was get on that plane. Once on that plane with the door shut, I knew I would be safe. I kept walking and never looked back.

People were still looking at me. I kept my head down and went to my seat. I hoped no one would ask any questions. The dam will break, and I won't be able to hold in my emotions. *How am I going to hold in my emotions until I get to Carol? Just don't make eye contact! You have only 45 minutes, and you will be with Carol.*

***

Carol was waiting for me at the airport, and as soon as we made eye contact, the dam erupted. All my built-up emotions came crashing out.

"What is wrong with you?" Carol asked.

I was crying so hard that my words were broken.

She was shocked as I exploded with details of all the things that James had done and of all the things that I had been going through. Carol and I drove around for a couple of hours for me to get myself together. Carol was afraid that her husband would not allow me to go on the trip if he knew how emotional I was. I finally pulled myself together and settled down. I was only able to do this by the grace of God.

Carol took me to my room and told her husband that I was tired and would join them later. He was okay with that. It gave me more needed time to get my thoughts together, pray, and focus on what God wanted me to do on this wonderful trip. A calm feeling came over me. I knew in my heart that I was going to be all right. We had the one day here before we went on to Atlanta, and from there on to Michigan to meet the rest of the team.

The next morning, we were on our way to the Atlanta airport. We gathered together all of our boxes of supplies. Carol's husband, the founder of the mission trip, knew how to get things organized. Each one of the team was allowed to have two seventy-pound boxes of supplies for the pastors and the people of the church. What a blessing this was going to be for all of us who were going to be a part of such a mission trip!

Once we arrived in Michigan, we were met by the other team members. They were just as excited as we were to be going on this trip. We all got in a circle and had a word of prayer for our safety and for us to be a blessing to others.

***

I had never seen a plane as big as this one in my life. It was two stories high and ten seats wide. We would be in the air for fourteen hours, and when we arrived in Japan, we had to change planes almost immediately.

The time advanced forward about twelve hours. We slept on the long flight, arrived in Japan, and traveled on to the Philippines. Once we arrived in the Philippines, our hosting families welcomed us with enthusiasm. Everything was prepared for us at a house on a lake. The house was set right on the banks of the China Sea. It was breathtaking to look over the sea and watch the tides, which were so far out that many of the people gathered shells and different things to sell at their local markets.

I knew that I was going to learn lots from this trip. I already knew that my participation would be a blessing to many people, but also I knew that I was the one being blessed by these wonderful people.

We settled in and started our work the next morning. The pastor and his wife made soup for the feeding center. It was hard to imagine what I would see. Once we arrived at the center, children were already standing in line with their containers, some bigger than others, to receive the soup. When they held up their containers to be filled, their eyes said it all. No words had to be uttered. We fed them physically and spiritually.

The first week went by quickly. We planned a trip to another island. For that trip, we had to ride a couple hours in a boat to get there. We would attend a pastors' conference, at which all the supplies we had collected would be given to the pastors of the other churches around the area. I had no clue what was in store for us when we got there. This island was known to be an island of witch doctors and voodooists. As we prepared for the service, you could hear the sounds of their practices in the distance.

But we were not going to let that deter us from what we were there for—to praise and worship the Lord and give Him praise and glory. As the sing teams sang and the interpreters shared their language, the service was under way—and was a wonderful service. We served with God's purpose and worked with other pastors. We stayed two nights on the island, and it was quite different to hear the sounds in the distance.

By beginning of our third week, I couldn't believe how quickly time had passed. We had so many experiences, and we had planned an outdoor meeting service tonight. By the time we started to go there, it was getting dark, and the smell was almost unbearable. We had hankies that we sprayed with perfume and held over our noses and mouths so that we could walk over the ditches to get to the stage. People were walking and carrying large pieces of wood. Many of the people had walked all day to attend the service, and they used the wood to sit on. And we struggle to sit on padded pews for a couple of hours! To see these people give their lives to the Lord and be part of the worship, reaching out their hands in praise, was such a blessing to me, and I was so thankful to be a part of it all.

I was so humbled by this trip. I came to be a blessing to them, but I was the one being blessed by them. Not only did I better appreciate air conditioning, but the showers were in a little place. We had to use a small dipper to pour water onto ourselves. To brush our teeth, we used bottled water that we had brought with us. All of this made for a life-changing experience for me and one I would never forget.

With two days left before we were to leave, we were told that we could go shopping to buy souvenirs. We went to the market on what they call a tri-taxi, a moped with three seats on back. It was quite a ride. We had a great time in the market.

We all had mixed emotions about saying good-bye, but we all knew that none of us was the same. This would be a lifelong memory. As the last evening rolled around, food was set on the table. Everyone was so proud to serve us. I jokingly told someone that I liked the 'fat off of the pork,' and to play a prank on me, a whole roasted hog's head was set in front of me. Everyone laughed at the surprised expression on my face. But I just laughed, picked up a knife, and cut a piece off the jaw and took a bite. Everyone started clapping their hands and laughing. Before the evening was over, the whole head was gone. All was good.

CHAPTER 14

The next day, we headed back home. On our way to the airport, we were all sort of quiet in our own ways and for our own reasons. For me, I wondered what I would have to face and what would be waiting there for me. I knew that I had been renewed in my spirit and strength. I believed and trusted that I was in God's hands and that he would protect me from all evil.

Once in Japan, we boarded the plane and knew that our flight back to the States would take around fourteen hours, and we had to adjust to the time change again. This meant that I would be home tomorrow. I wasn't sure I wanted that. A part of me did want to go home, but a part of me was concerned about what waited for me there.

The trip back home was pretty quick for me. Maybe it was because of dread, but it seemed that in no time, Carol was taking me to the airport for my flight home. Three weeks had passed, but I still recalled vividly the situation that I left.

As my flight landed, I began to feel sick at my stomach. I wanted to be excited to see James, but I just did not know what to expect from him. I was so nervous.

I saw him. James walked over to me, put his arms around me, and kissed me. "I'm glad that you're home," he said.

I was glad to be home too. On the way home, I tried to share some of my trip with him, but he didn't want to hear about it. James wanted to tell me all the things that he had done while I was gone. So, I just closed down and listened to what he had to say.

"I didn't get anything done around the condo," James said.

"That's okay. It's the first of October, and I can finish unpacking boxes and decorate for fall at the same time," I answered.

We didn't talk much the rest of the way home. I was so tired with jet lag, I just wanted to rest. By morning, I was feeling the time change. But to my surprise James didn't go to work. He had taken a couple of weeks off. What was he up to? But at this point, all I wanted to do was sleep and rest. James kept coming in the bedroom, waking me, and starting his nonsense on me again.

"Who were you with on your trip?"

"How many men did you sleep with?"

God, please help me through this.

It was the same old thing, just a new day. I tried to ignore it. I told James that I wanted to buy some fall flowers and start decorating. I wanted to go by the church to share with them the wonderfulness of the trip, but I knew that would have to wait.

"You want to buy some flowers? I'll take you," James said.

I wanted to go purchase the flowers myself. I just wanted to be by myself and visit my friends. I knew that was not going to happen.

"Well, maybe later," I said. I decided to wait a few days and see what happened.

"I want to take you someplace this evening," James said.

"Where?" I asked.

"I'm not going to tell you," he answered. "You'll find out later."

So, flashbacks cluttered my mind and I became gripped with fear and was scared. Where was he taking me? What was in his mind?

I started praying and asking God for His safety and guidance as the day slipped into the evening. I kept believing that James was taking me out of town for a nice dinner.

I got dressed and walked out of the bedroom. I was standing at the top of the stairs, and I clearly heard God's voice and His words to me, "Stand still and let Me fight this battle. It is bigger than you are."

What was God telling me?

"Yes, Lord," I answered aloud and continued to walk down the stairs and out the door to the car.

I got in the car, and James pulled out in a direction that confused me. I wasn't sure where we were headed. I didn't say anything. I didn't ask any questions. My mind was spinning with questions—*Where? Why? What?*

We ended up at a place that was sort of like a diner. When we went inside, there was a woman there. We sat down with her, and we just looked at each other.

James looked at me and then looked at her and asked, "Did you know that my wife is going out with your boyfriend?"

What did I just hear him say? I was stunned!

"No," the woman calmly said. "I don't think that she would do that. She is a good woman. You must be confused on that."

I thought, *Oh my! You have no idea how confused he is on that and other things! If you only knew!*

I understood now what God was telling me. He was right. This situation was much bigger than I could handle. *What was James going to do next?*

I had a sickening feeling run through me. I was numb. I had so many mixed emotions, I couldn't even react. My head was spinning. I thought that I was losing my mind and that this was the last push. It was a point of no return. But I knew if the Enemy got my mind, I would forever be trapped with no way out.

I silently prayed. *God I am totally in your hands. Your word says: No weapon formed against you shall prosper. (Isaiah 54:17 NKJV) I stand on the Word.*

Deliver me, O Lord, from the evil man. Psalms 140:1 NKJV

This continues to be my prayer today.

***

For the next few weeks, I couldn't go anywhere or do anything without James being right there with me. It was so strange. James had never wanted to do anything with me before, and now, he was always by my side. Every waking moment, James was constant in his aggravation of me.

I was so beaten down. I still hadn't unpacked some things from the move, and I really didn't care about much of anything at this point. I was just going through the motions of things. I always tried to make sure that no one knew that anything was wrong or what was going on behind the closed doors.

Sometimes you never know what does go on in someone else's home. There's a story behind every face, but you may only know what they want you to know. Hidden secrets could be there. I had plenty of hidden secrets, especially since anyone who met James and me thought that we were the perfect couple. Only a few knew the hidden story.

We had planned a birthday party for one of the grandchildren. On the day of the party, James backed the van into a mailbox. He became very upset and blamed me for his backing into the mailbox. I wasn't helping him look and watch where he was going.

Surprisingly, James didn't insist that we go back home. He looked at the damage and decided that he could fix it. We went inside to a house full of people, and I just knew that at any time, he would erupt, start a big fight, and ruin the whole day for all there. Thank God, he didn't.

It appeared that he had a good time. On the way home, he even talked about how nice the party was and how happy it made him. I was surprised to hear him say something positive for a change. He was mostly negative about so many things.

We got back home and settled in for the night. We watched TV, and things seemed okay.

"I think that the van needs to go into the shop to be checked out," James said.

"I think that's a good idea," I answered.

"It is after ten," James said. "Let's go to bed."

I knew that he wanted to have sex. So, when we went to bed, it was obvious that I did not want sex. But I did not want to cause an argument, so I just went through the motions of having sex. It seemed so strange. He seemed to be satisfied, and that was what mattered to him. I just turned over, cried for a while, and finally fell off to sleep.

Out of the silence, a sound woke me. It was early in the morning, about 4:30 am.

"Did you hear that?" I asked James as I turned to his side of the bed.

James wasn't there. I was surprised that he was not in bed.

The noise was so loud and was like nothing I had ever heard before. I jumped to my feet and ran to the door. When I opened the door, I couldn't believe my eyes.

Oh my God! What has happened? Blood and flesh were everywhere—the walls, the floor, up to ceiling! It was a war zone. I smelled gunpowder and blood. What had happened?

James had shot himself.

I walked by James to get to the phone. I could see him lying in a hump, face down. He wasn't moving. I called 911.

I tried to get to James, but it was as if there was a clear shield around him. I could not get through it. I passed by him twice—once to get to the phone, and once to open the door for the paramedics.

"Oh, James, what have you done?"

I was in complete state of shock. I recall looking at James, and all I could see was the back of him with his white T-shirt with no blood. But there was blood and tissue everywhere. When the paramedics arrived, I heard someone say, "We're going to have to pry the phone from her hands."

I had clenched the only thing solid at that moment. Someone walked me downstairs. That was the last time I would see or be in that condo.

As I waited outside, I felt the coldness in the air. It was a foggy October morning. Someone brought me a blanket and wrapped it around me. The police arrived, and one of the officers walked over to me to ask me questions.

"Ma'am, I need to check your clothing," the officer said.

"What?" I questioned.

"I need to check your clothing," the officer repeated.

I didn't understand. Why was he checking me? I hadn't done anything.

"Please open up the blanket," he said.

I opened my blanket, and the officer shined this big light on top of my head to the bottom of my feet.

"She's clean," he yelled.

He took me by the arm and walked me to the police car. He then put me in the back of the car. I guess that was the last straw in feeling trapped for things that I didn't do. I completely fell apart. I was told that I went crazy. I started kicking the seat and door and yelling for them to let me out. Thank God, about that time, Dee showed up. When Dee walked toward the car, the police officer let me out of the car to go with her. I ran so hard that I almost knocked her down. We both just sat on the sidewalk until I was told that I needed to leave.

Before James's body was brought out, he was pronounced dead at the scene.

By now, Sue and her husband were there, as well as my brother Red and his family. Several other people were there, too. Carol was on her way from Tennessee. It was daylight, and I needed a place to stay. I chose to go to Dee's place. My brother Will and his family from Florida were on their way.

I needed help with everything. What should I to do with my things? What about funeral arrangements?

The next day I had to go to the funeral home and make all the arrangements for the service. I didn't realize how some things just fall into place and other things require quick decisions. Everything went pretty smoothly because of my family and friends. They were always at my side, watching out for me.

His daughter's mother wanted to attend the service. I told her that as long as no one caused a scene that I thought that it would be okay. I thank God for giving me the grace, mercy, and softness in my heart to accept her request.

Under the circumstances, the service was beautiful in every way. I had never seen so many people attend a funeral. After the service, family, friends, and I went to my brother's Red's home. We had great fellowship and prayer time. God brought deliverance and calm to a raging storm. I shared some things with the group, and it was a way of mourning. I know that God Himself sheltered me and carried me in his arms around that condo. I know this because God protected me from getting any blood on me. It was a miracle. Everyone there was shocked to see that I had no blood on me. None. It was miracle. It was God's miracle in protecting me. I'm forever thankful.

Sue, her husband, my brothers Red and Will, and others helped with removing my things and putting them in storage. Carol told me God awoke her with instructions on what she needed to do to help me. She and Red went with me to the funeral home and acquired the death certificate. What normally would have taken weeks to obtain, we were able to obtain in one day. We also went to the bank to take care of the financial side of things. I never had a checking account. I had always been told that I wasn't smart enough to have one.

"What I am going to do?" I asked.

"You are moving in with me," Carol said.

What to do with the van? What to do with James's things? There were loose ends on so many things.

By the first of November, I had settled in with Carol. On November 15, I was going to be 50 years old. To my surprise, a big birthday party was planned. My brothers, sisters, friends, and other family members came. It was more a celebration of being alive. Everyone knew that I was still trying to adjust to my new surroundings and to move forward on my own. I stayed in prayer, asking for guidance and direction. I attended different churches with Carol and her husband and went with them wherever they evangelized. I enjoyed doing this. I could feel myself growing in the Spirit again. I began to feel the joy that only God can give. I knew that God was healing me, and He didn't want me to be a bitter and angry woman the rest of my life. I didn't want that either. I began to realize how different my life was going to be without the verbal abuse. *What a difference it will make in my life!*

***

NEW YEAR

My brother-in-law received a call asking him to accept a pastoral position at a church in Fort Myers, Florida. He went into prayer and fasting, asking God to provide him direction and guidance. He and Carol were asked to have a weekend service. He explained my situation to the church and asked that I be allowed to join them. I was invited and welcomed. We went to Florida for the weekend service, and it was a blessing.

Back in Tennessee, a week later, a couple from the church took me back to Indiana to Red's house, where I visited with all my friends and family.

I picked up my van so I that would have my own vehicle to travel. I wanted to stop and visit with a couple from Tennessee, with whom I had remained lifelong friends. I would be saying goodbye to all my friends in Indiana, so I thought seeing them would be perfect timing. This trip to

Tennessee would be a first for me. Driving by myself to Chattanooga was a first for me. I had never taken a trip alone. I was finding out that I was facing doing a lot of things alone and on my own. It was revitalizing for me to know that I could do things.

When I got back at Carol's, packing already had begun. No one was wasting time. I had only one room of stuff, so packing for me was pretty quick. Since we were making a long-distance move, some men from Florida arrived to help with the packing, loading, and driving of the truck. It was amazing how quickly things were packed and ready to go. When it was time for us to head out, my nephew rode with me to keep me company along the way.

The trip was long, but we finally arrived at the parsonage. Several people from the church were waiting for us. From the food in the kitchen cabinets to rooms prepared for our arrival, everything was set in place. Meals were prepared for us, we settled in, and it felt like it was family. What a welcome! We were so excited, and we were so thankful for God showing us where we needed to be. We knew we had arrived.

CHAPTER 15

MY NEW BEGINNING
FLORIDA, MARCH 2001

What is this year going to hold for me? Finally settled in, I decided to go to a vocational school of nursing. I took summer school classes to prepare for the nursing program. After being out of school for 30 years, I needed some refresher classes.

I finished summer school and entered the fall nursing class. I thought it would be so easy since I had worked as a certified nursing assistant all those years, but I was in for a rude awakening. It wasn't easy, but I was determined.

I thanked God for my family support and my wonderful Auntie. My Auntie listened to my cries, with happy tears and sad tears. Auntie was one of my Prayer Warriors. Sometimes I would call her and tell her that I did not want to go to school.

"Now, sweetie, you have to," Auntie would say. I would pick up my books and head on out the door. I knew what I had to do and that was to pull up my boot-straps and bury myself in school.

Even though my mind still needed healing from the tragedy, I knew that God would give me a sound mind and the strength to go through whatever was ahead of me. God directed me to Florida and put me among people He knew would support to me. I was here to be supported and to offer support to others.

One of my instructor-teachers knew how my husband had died. She confided in me about her own attempt to take her life.

"I believe God sent you here for me to give me encouragement," she said.

I instantly remembered when I asked God, "What do you want me to learn from all this?" I knew that was part of it. I was there to listen and to speak about my experience. I was there for encouragement. She thanked me often and always smiled.

I do believe that we are individuals, and we go through things in our lives to help others along the way. I always said, "We all have a story."

At this point one more year before graduating from school. I never realized how demanding I would find school to be.

By spring, my brother-in-law had purchased a white-on-white convertible car for his used car lot. I wanted so much to drive that car, so we worked out an agreement that allowed me to own it. I loved putting the top down, cranking up the radio on the oldies station, and cruising across the big bridge in town. Sometimes I took kids from church for rides. They loved it.

Spring break was over, and I was back to school. A couple of months had gone by. One Saturday I decided to go for a ride. I stopped at a gas station, but I couldn't get the button inside to open the door on the tank. I decided to run up to the parsonage to see my brother-in-law. As I pulled into the parking lot, I saw one of the brothers in the church sitting in his truck. I pulled up beside him. I noticed that he laid something down on the seat. I figured it was his cell phone, since he was always talking on it. He rolled down his window, and I proceeded to tell him of my problem. He got out of his truck and walked over to my car. I opened up the door, and when he touched the button, the lid popped open with no hesitation.

"What did you do?" I asked.

"Nothing," he answered. "It works just fine."

I thanked him and went on my way.

***

On Sunday morning, I felt such an excitement in the air. I thought *We're going to have a good service today.* I loved being a part of the choir, and

I was looking forward to singing the new song we had practiced. Carol was the Praise and Worship leader, and she was doing a super job.

When I arrived and walked into the sanctuary. The presence of the Lord could be felt. *Thank you, God, have your way.* As the service started, some people were giving testimonies of what God had done for them this past week. The brother who had helped me with my gas tank stood up and said, "I need to tell you what God did for me this week." Everyone became very quiet.

"Yesterday, on Saturday," he said, "I was sitting in my truck in the church parking lot. I was sitting there with a gun in my mouth, ready to pull the trigger, when I looked up. All I could see was what looked like a band of angels coming up behind me. I realized it was Tawana in her white car. At that moment, I laid down the gun on the seat. She started telling what was going on, and she needed help with the gas lock on her car. I got out to help her. Nothing appeared wrong with it, and it worked as soon as I pushed it. Tawana went on her way, not knowing that God had sent her at that very minute to save my life."

He continued to say, "I know He used her in a simple way, but it was her timing. It was God's timing. God is on time."

I now knew why that all happened. I had never had any trouble with that button before, nor did I have any trouble after that. I thank God for His using me for his purpose.

The service was a very powerful one after that testimonial. It was clear to me that miracles happen. I still believe in miracles, don't you?

***

SEPTEMBER 11, 2001

I was sitting on my sofa, going over last-minute homework, and half watching *The Today Show*. I saw the plane go into one of the twin towers. I was in shock, as was the rest of the world. We all were in shock. Classes were cancelled for several days. It was such a tragedy, and my heart was in pain for all the people.

Back in school, it was a struggle—more on some days than others. I worked hard, and I was hanging in there. In class, I heard that one of my classmates needed a car. I knew that she had two or three children, and she was in need of help. I thought of a few people in our church family who might be willing to help. She was a Godly woman, and I was sure that someone in her church family would help her get to school and church. *God will provide.*

A couple of weeks went by, and one night God woke me up and said, "You need to help your classmate."

I said out loud, "But my car is a little car." I started to pray about it. When God speaks, we should listen. The more I prayed about it, it became clearer what I was to do. I wanted to be obedient to what God wanted me to do.

I wondered how many people God had dealt with about this, and people shrugged it off. I didn't want to miss my blessing, so I was going to listen to God's words. I went to my brother-in-law and told him what I needed to do.

"Are you sure?" he asked.

"I have never been surer of anything I've ever done before," I answered.

"I have a big Chevrolet Caprice on the car lot. I need to trade my fun car even for that car, with no strings attached, paid in full, and a clear title. I will give it to this woman," my brother-in-law said. "I will get everything in order for you." A week later, it was ready.

I called her and told her to come to the church parsonage because I had something she might be able to use. She and her mom came by. We started with prayer about trusting that God will provide, and we were all in agreement. I started telling her how God had dealt with me regarding her situation for several weeks. "I want to give you the keys to this car. It is yours. Paid in full, with a clear title, and it is free to you."

"What?!" She couldn't believe what I was telling her. She and her mom just started shouting right there in the yard. She called her Dad.

"Dad, this woman just gave me a car!" she said.

"What's wrong with it?" he asked. "Nobody just gives anybody a car!"

God is so good! I realized then that the little car was really not my fun car as I had thought, but it was to be used to save another man's life and be a blessing.

***

GRADUATION

My graduation was hard-earned. I was so excited and felt so proud of myself. I had a beautiful graduation with all my family and friends there. Immediately after graduation, I started work. I worked at an assisted-living facility, and I loved it. I worked there for about a year and moved to another city, Bradenton. I worked there at a skilled nursing facility. It was really a nice place to work. I watched myself come out of all the torment. I had never realized my potential or imagined what I could do on my own. I am the person I am today by the grace of God.

"I can do all things through Christ who strengthens me." Philippians 4:13 KJV

Yes, I can!

I worked as a licensed nurse and was nominated by my peers to take a supervisor position. After a vacation with family, I accepted the position for a 60-day trail basis. But I had found my niche and worked there for six years as supervisor.

LIFE TODAY

Looking back on my life, who would have thought that I could have achieved so many things in my life? I owe it all to God who gave me a sound mind and a loving heart. It took me two years to really and truly forgive my husband for all those things he put me through. At that time, I visited the cemetery and sat down at his gravesite. I began to cry and pray.

"God, help me to forgive and to move on with my life," I prayed. "I know that this is what you want me to do."

I guess I must have been there for a couple of hours when I felt this wonderful release come over me. I knew that my heart was free. I truly had forgiven James.

"Thank you, God, and it is only by your Grace I am really free in my mind, heart, and spirit."

I followed God's lead and moved to Tennessee. I love it here. I have met so many wonderful people, and I'm able to be there for my Auntie. I continue my nursing in geriatrics and assisted living.

***

I WOULD LIKE TO PROVIDE A FEW SHORT SCRIPTURE VERSES THAT WERE AND ARE IMPORTANT TO ME:

"For this very night stood by my side an angel of God." Acts 27:23–24

"God's peace which passeth all understanding" Philippians 4:7

"Make a way to escape." 1 Corinthians 10:13

"No weapon formed against me shall prosper." Isaiah 54:17

"Deliver me O Lord from the evil man." Psalms 140:1

"God is our refuge and strength." Psalms 46:1

"I can do all things through Christ..." Philippians 4:13

"With God, all things are possible." Matthew 19:26

INSPIRATIONAL MOMENTS

All the crosses you bear will build you a platform to stand on.

They say time has a way of healing all wounds, but it only forms scar tissue to better cover the pain.

The body will forget what it feels, but the mind never forgets what it hears.

Only look back to see how far you have come.

Scars remind us where we've been; they don't dictate where we are going.

Tawana Campbell's childhood home is a one-stoplight town in sleepy southern Indiana. At the age of 16, Campbell left home to be married. Like that of many of her classmates and other women of her generation, Campbell's dream was to be 'the perfect wife and homemaker.' But dreams sometimes are far from reality, and Campbell refused to succumb as her dream morphed into nightmare. With determination and a firm faith in God, Campbell learned how to drive, earned her GED, became a licensed cosmetologist, and finally found her niche in geriatric nursing. She is the proud auntie of several beautiful but spoiled nieces and nephews. *Shattered But Not Broken* is Campbell's first publication.